MIND, CULTURE, AND ACTIVITY

AN INTERNATIONAL JOURNAL

EDITORS

HARRY DANIELS
University of Birmingham, England

ANNE EDWARDS
University of Birmingham, England

MICHAEL COLE
University of California, San Diego

YRJÖ ENGESTRÖM
University of California, San Diego

JAMES V. WERTSCH
Washington University

Editorial Board

T0271895

PHILIP AGRE
University of California, Los Angeles

LUIS MOLL
University of Arizona

AMELIA ÁLVAREZ
University of Salamanca

TEREZINHA NUNES
Oxford Brookes University

KIYOSHI AMANO
Chuo University

CAROL PADDEN
University of California, San Diego

DAVID BAKHURST
Queen's University

ANNE MARIE PALINCSAR
University of Michigan

KING BEACH
Michigan State University

ANNE NELLY PERRET-CLEMONT
Institut de Psychologie

SUSANNE BØDKER
Aarhus University

CLOTILDE PONTECORVO
University of Rome

ALESSANDRO DURANTI
University of California, Los Angeles

GRACIELA QUINTEROS
Universidad Autónoma Metropolitana

EVA EKEBLAD
Sweden

BARBARA ROGOFF
University of California, Santa Cruz

CHARLES GOODWIN
University of California, Los Angeles

ROGER SÄLJÖ
University of Linköping

GIYOO HATANO
University of the Air

FALK SEEGER
Universitaet Bielefeld

MARIANE HEDEGAARD
University of Aarhus

ANA LUIZA BUSTAMENTE SMOLKA
State University of Campinas

EDWIN HUTCHINS
University of California, San Diego

SUSAN LEIGH STAR
University of California, San Diego

VERA JOHN–STEINER
University of New Mexico

ANNA STETSENKO
City University of New York

VICTOR KAPTELININ
Umeå University

CHARLES TOLMAN
University of Victoria

ALFRED LANG
University of Bern

NAOKI UENO
National Institute for Educational Research

JEAN LAVE
University of California, Berkeley

JAAN VALSINER
Clark University

CAROL LEE
Northwestern University

OLGA A. VÁSQUEZ
University of California, San Diego

DAVID MIDDLETON
Loughborough University

GORDON WELLS
University of California, Santa Cruz

BOOK REVIEW EDITOR: Anna Sfard
The University of Haifa, Israel

EDITORIAL COORDINATOR: Peggy Bengel
University of California, San Diego

Production Editor: Rebecca J. Vogt, *Lawrence Erlbaum Associates, Inc.*

Subscription Information: *Mind, Culture, and Activity* is published quarterly by Lawrence Erlbaum Associates, Inc.

First published 2003 by Lawrence Erlbaum Associates, Inc.

Published 2016 by Routledge
2 Park Square, Milton Park, Abingdon, Oxon OX14 4RN
711 Third Avenue, New York, NY 10017, USA

Routledge is an imprint of the Taylor & Francis Group, an informa business

ISBN 13: 978-1-57958-076-6 (pbk)

MIND, CULTURE, AND ACTIVITY. *10*(1), 1–2

INTRODUCTION

Culture, Technology, and Development: In Memory of Jan Hawkins

Michael Cole

University of California, San Diego

On behalf of the editors, it is a privilege to bring to our readers a set of articles written by former colleagues and friends of Jan Hawkins, whose untimely death serves as the sad occasion that motivates the diverse set of scholarly articles you are about to encounter. As Louis Gomez and Roy Pea note in their introduction, Jan was a member of an outstandingly talented group of graduate students who participated in the weekly seminars held in what was then referred to as The Institute for Comparative Human Development during the mid-1970s.

If there was a single theme that brought together this amazingly diverse group of scholars and that dominates both the substantive articles you are about to read and the several commentaries written about them by people who worked closely with Jan in the last decades of her life, it was the belief in the value of human diversity, not only as a resource for understanding human nature, but as a necessity for continued human development. We worked then, as now, in an environment that routinely turned difference into deficit and that held up unexamined, ethnocentric, biases as the criterion against which to judge, and design programs for, those who did not fit the dominant ideology of then-and-still dominant social groups in American society. Our common enemy, then, as now, was the social creation of social inequality. Our common goal was the creation of an effective, human alternative to dominant disciplinary practices that would make diversity a resource for human development and not a problem.

Such an undertaking could not succeed without creating a group which itself was representative of the diversity of the social groups with which it sought to work. As a consequence, the group that came together in these seminars was perhaps the most diverse group of scholars, along almost any dimension one cares to assess them, ever to come together in an American academic institution.

Although Rockefeller University provided unique resources for such an undertaking, it also posed unique impediments. In particular, its social organization, modeled on European natural science laboratories of the early 20th century, did not provide career opportunities for anyone other than the person who headed the laboratory. The attendant contradictions and the pressures

Requests for reprints should be sent to Michael Cole, Laboratory of Comparative Human Cognition, University of California, San Diego, La Jolla, CA 92093–0092.

they produced could not be avoided, and as a consequence the Institute was closed in 1978 and its members scattered across the country.

Fortunately, like a dandelion on a summer breeze, the seeds of that unique group took root in many places and their progeny continue to multiply, diversify, and propagate. As the articles and commentaries you are about to read testify, the ideas, practices, and values that Jan Hawkins helped to create in the mid-1970s are now to be found around the world. A more fitting tribute to her generative, generous, creativity, would be difficult to imagine.

MIND. CULTURE. AND ACTIVITY. *10*(1), 3–8

ARTICLES

Technology, Culture, and Adaptive Minds: An Introduction

Xiaodong Lin

Teachers College
Columbia University

Giyoo Hatano

Human Development and Education Program
The University of the Air

This special issue, inspired by the spirit of Jan Hawkins, focuses on ways that our knowledge of technology, culture, and adaptive minds can be brought together to create new opportunities for learning and personal growth. Jan cared deeply about these issues and explored them in her own work and in her travels throughout the world. She was one of the first to call our attention to the social and equity issues around the design and uses of technologies (Spiro & Collins, 1999). Her research style included helping people from different disciplines connect with one another personally and electronically to solve common problems. The special issue will follow her lead by exploring in detail issues such as what roles technology plays in human learning and cultural change, how diverse cultural contexts interact with a new technology to produce varied outcomes, and ways in which human minds adapt themselves to technology as well as adapt technology to them.

The four articles in this special issue represent new research efforts that explore how cultures can influence and learn from one another through the technological artifacts they exchange and sometimes co-develop. The technological artifacts involved in these studies range from physical houses and procedures for building them to computer software and 3-D virtual worlds. We view these artifacts as closely associated with particular cultural practices, not as material and symbolic entities separate from their cultural contexts. As such, exchanging and co-constructing technological artifacts often implies exchanging and co-constructing a particular set of cultural values and practices (Lin, 2001). When these values contrast with another, such exchange may make invisi-

Requests for reprints should be sent to Xiaodong Lin, Department of Mathematics, Science and Technology, Teachers College, Columbia University, 525 West 120th Street Box 8, New York, NY 10027. E-mail: xlin@tc.columbia.edu

ble cultural needs and beliefs explicit, and may also precipitate (often unplanned) changes in responsibilities, roles, and practices.

The special issue explores the role of technology as a catalyst for changes in classroom culture and as a mediator for new forms of human interactions and learning. Two of the articles look at technology in cross-cultural settings, and the other two articles consider technology in the context of a sub-culture within a larger culture. Jointly, they present a picture of how people adapt technology to meet their diverse needs, while they adapt their educational practices to respond to the technologies.

TECHNOLOGICAL ARTIFACTS AS A CATALYST FOR CHANGE

Throughout history, technologies have served as powerful catalysts for change, whether introduced from within a culture (e.g., the printing press; Eisenstein, 1979) or from another culture (e.g., the snow machine; Pelto & Muller-Wille, 1987). They can produce unpredictable changes, which include both challenges and opportunities for human learning and development. This is in part due to their secondary effects, a few examples of which are given in the following. At the individual level, a new tool often requires learners to master a new set of skills, whereas making the skills for using its predecessor obsolete (Wertsch, 1995). As a result, people develop new knowledge about their own abilities to think and solve problems. At the interpersonal level, a new tool may change the power relationships among people, such as relations between teachers and students, explored in the studies by Schofield and Davidson ("The Impact of Internet Use on Relationships between Teachers and Students"), and by Lin and Schwartz ("Reflection At the Crossroads of Cultures"). These power shifts in classrooms may be related to the fact that modern technology often deprives experts of their privileged status by redefining the expertise needed to accomplish academic or occupational tasks. A new tool may also create new folk models and ideals. For example, such notions as the "barrier-free environment" and "equal opportunity employer" that apply at the community level are greatly enhanced, if not induced, by the invention of the wheel chair.

A new tool tends to influence people's life beyond its enhanced efficiency in achieving specific goals, in part due to its unanticipated extended uses. Even though the design of a new tool is originally embedded in a particular practice, it is often used in other contexts, sometimes in ways, which its designers never imagined—for example, the Amazon.com web-site can be used to find book citations.

Another notion shared by all four articles is that technology is rarely "culture free" in the sense that it brings about homogenous changes in all cultural contexts. How a new tool influences peoples' lives, positively or negatively, depends on how it is introduced and incorporated. A modern mass-production technology may sweep away local, indigenous technologies, or both types of technologies may coexist, each serving different users and varied needs. We would like to emphasize that what a new tool brings about depends on the interaction between the tool's intrinsic properties and the prior culture of the people who use it, or more specifically, the already existing set of tools, beliefs, and practices. Adaptive minds can often find a good match between a tool and the local cultural context through improvisation and reflection. The work by Lee ("Toward a Framework for the Design of Culturally Responsive Digital Environments") strongly suggests that to be successful a new technology should be "responsive" to the needs, strengths, and values of the learners when introduced into classrooms. Technology design should leave space for different cultures to build on their strengths and to adapt the technology to their culture. This space will allow, for example, individual teachers and students explicitly to choose aspects of an artifact for use and reflect upon their choices.

These considerations imply that only flexible artifacts are likely to be effectively applied to many different cultural contexts (Lin & Hatano, 2002; Schwartz, Lin, Brophy & Bransford, 1999), because the needed adaptations cannot be predicted ahead of time and must be improvised on the spot. This is particularly true in classroom settings, owing to the dynamic interactions that characterize them. On-the-spot adaptation requires users and designers to be open-minded about uncertainties and to seize emerging learning opportunities. Therefore, the changes observed when technologies are successfully introduced into classrooms are the result of adaptation made through ingenious improvisation and careful reflection as well as decision making by the local teachers and students. Although every technology is likely to be accompanied by both positive and negative outcomes (e.g., cars bring pollution as well as rapid access to distant places), these outcomes will be modulated by the existing classroom culture.

Understanding the interaction of the tool and the sociocultural context will provide clues for the humanistic uses of new technologies. The articles collected in this special issue reveal this improvising and reflective adaptation process (Hatano & Inagaki, 1986), where teachers and students adapt technology to meet their diverse classroom needs, while adapting their educational practices to take advantage of the affordances offered by the technology—a bi-directional adaptation process.

TECHNOLOGIES AS MEDIATORS FOR NEW FORM OF HUMAN INTERACTIONS

Technological artifacts "re-mediate" interactions among people and their environment, so that people can do things that would be more difficult to do without them (Cole, 1996). For example, global telecommunications technology permits cross-cultural exchanges that would be far more slow and quite difficult otherwise (many children and teachers do not live under conditions that make such contacts likely to happen). Internet technologies *potentially* allow contact with a wider variety of other cultures and expertise than face-to-face meetings, affording new opportunities for reflection. Two of the current papers pay close attention to the kinds of learning and reflection that occur when people interact with people from cultures other than their own (see Hammond "Building Houses, Building Lives"; Lin and Schwartz, "Reflection at the Crossroads of Cultures"). In the first case the interaction is mediated through face-to-face interactions in co-constructing school–community gardens and houses; in the second case the interaction is mediated through the use of the Internet and 3-D virtual technologies.

These studies reveal that exposure to different cultural values and practices may make invisible cultural needs and beliefs more visible, so that deeper learning and revision of core values will occur. For example, the cultural interaction involved in Hammond's study created rich opportunities where teachers, children and parents from different cultural backgrounds had to communicate and negotiate over their different principles and practices. Such interaction was so dynamic that many unplanned conflicts in cultural values and practices arose throughout the process of the collaboration. These conflicts forced all parties to learn to resolve their differences and to create space for all to contribute, as they worked together toward common educational goals. Most valuable were the situations in which people discussed the choices they made, and why they made them.

Facilitating cultural interaction with the help of technologies is a very delicate business. Simply putting people of different cultures in contact does not guarantee that their learning experiences will be positive and helpful. Misunderstandings often result from cultural differences, and if left unattended, may negatively impact teachers' and students' attitudes toward people from other cultures (see Lin & Schwartz, this issue). These attitudes can hinder people from learning about other people and themselves. Lin and Schwartz explored how various forms of cultural interactions affect learning and reflection. Their work suggests that cultural interactions involved in creating joint artifacts and knowing each other as individuals creates a bond between members of different cultures and allows people from different cultures to discover their own strengths and weaknesses that would have remained invisible without such interaction.

The studies in this collection provide only an initial understanding of the learning potential offered by various types of technology-mediated cultural exchange. Questions remain about how to study new technologies, especially when many of the cultural and educational outcomes are not predicable by the designers and educators.

THE ARTICLES

Each article in this issue attempts to explore these challenges in detail. In the first article, Lorie Hammond ("Building Houses, Building Lives") presents a field study in which mainstream American teachers, assisted by a Laotian student teacher, worked with American and Laotian parents to build a garden and field house as part of an urban school–community science curriculum project. The initial goal of the project was cultural heritage preservation for Southeast Asian elementary school children and their families. However, the process of working together through the building of a concrete technology, a field house and a school garden, enabled both parties to develop trustful relationships and to construct a new joint culture, neither Laotian nor American, but influenced by both. It is through experiencing the ways in which each group approached the technology of building a house and planting a garden that each could see the other and could adapt to new practices. Too often, multicultural projects deal with idealized versions of cultures, as told through stories and accounts. Concrete technologies, which are shared between cultures—such as house building—can often communicate different cultural values and practices in an explicit manner.

The second article by Carol Lee ("Toward a Framework for the Design of Culturally Responsive Digital Environments") looks at changes in literacy practices induced by the use of computer-based software tools designed to support students to develop literacy reasoning in response to canonical literature appropriate to African–American elementary and high school students. The paper uses cultural-historical activity theory as a lens for analyzing how students' reflective adaptation of each tool resulted in changes in students' learning. She examined not only the role of the mediating technological artifacts, but also the norms for social interaction, the intellectual quality of the literacy tasks, and the particular practices designed to support learning. Her findings indicate that as students interacted with the tools in two educational contexts, they employed language and communication patterns that are specific to African–American culture. She concludes the article by suggesting ways that educational technology might be designed to be "culturally responsive" and to leave room for all cultures to build on their strengths.

"The Impact of Internet Use on Relationships Between Teachers and Students"), also investigated the effects of computer-based technologies, but with the focus on changes in classroom roles and relationships they bring about. Schofield and Davidson carried out 5-year study of a major effort to bring the Internet to a large urban school district. They found that Internet use increased student autonomy, both in the classrooms of teachers (who had not planned this outcome) and in the classes of teachers who intentionally used the Internet to foster this change. Further, Internet use frequently resulted unexpectedly in warmer and less adversarial teacher–student relations, teachers' discovery of unexpected Internet skills on the part of students who had not otherwise impressed them, and teachers' new appreciation of the difficulty of learning as they themselves coped with the sometimes forgotten experience of mastering something new. Finally, a variety of new and generally unanticipated student roles emerged in high schools using the Internet, in which students served both as tutors for their teachers and as technical experts for their schools.

The final article by Xiaodong Lin and Dan Schwartz ("Reflection at the Crossroads of Cultures") describes the kinds of learning and reflection that occur as a result of different forms of interaction with technological artifacts and with individuals from cultures that differ from their own. They explored how interaction and learning can be accomplished both in person and virtually. Their work shows that when people engage a new culture, whether across oceans or classrooms, they experience an increase in reflection about their own identities, goals, and responsibilities. Because of its appearance in new cross-cultural contacts, reflection appears as a deeply social act. In addition, they identify two significant social functions of reflection. First, it helps people decide which cultural practices to appropriate and how to adapt them. Second, it helps people become more receptive to the presence of different values and practices. Their article presents several research instances in which technological artifacts are used to promote cross-cultural contact. In some cases, the artifact communicates culture because of the practices it suggests. In other cases, the technology helps people communicate directly about their values and practices. Based on their successes and failures, they offer a set of provisional design principles for technologies that encourage reflective learning through cross-cultural reflection.

The special issue concludes with the commentaries by Bransford and Cole, who consider some features that all the articles have in common and will share their thoughts about what the next steps should be to create a broader dialogue about how human learning can be enhanced by technology, cultural diversity, and improvising and reflective adaptation. In addition, several of Jan Hawkin's close colleagues, Margaret Honey and Allan Collins offer valuable insights as to how Jan would think about the kinds of work discussed in the special issue.

ACKNOWLEDGMENTS

The writing of this article was supported by the Small Spencer Grant, Spencer Foundation. The opinions expressed in the article are those of the authors and not the foundation.

REFERENCES

Cole, M. (1996). *Cultural psychology: A once and future discipline.* Cambridge: Harvard University Press.
Eisenstein, E. L. (1979). *The printing press as an agent of change: Communications and cultural transformations in early modern Europe.* New York: Cambridge University Press.

Hatano, G., & Inagaki, K. (1986). Two courses of expertise. In H. Stevenson, H. Azuma, & K. Hakuta (Eds.), *Child development and education in Japan* (pp. 262–272). New York: Freeman.

Lin, X. D. (2001). Reflective adaptation of a technology artifact: A case study of classroom change. *Cognition & Instruction, 19*(4), 395–440.

Lin, X. D., & Hatano, G. (2002). Cross–cultural adaptation of educational technology. In T. Koschmann, R. Hall, & N. Miyake (Eds.), *CSCL2: Carrying forward the conversation* (pp. 89–97). Hillsdale, NJ: Lawrence Erlbaum Associates, Inc.

Pelto, P. J., & Muller-Wille, L. (1987). Snowmobiles: Technological revolution in the Arctic. In H. R. Bernard & P. J. Pelto (Eds.), *Technology and social change* (pp. 207–258). Prospect Heights, IL: Waveland.

Schwartz, D. L., Brophy, S., Lin, X. D., & Bransford, J. D. (1999). Software for managing complex learning: Examples from an educational psychology course. *Educational Technology Research & Development, 47*(2), 39–59.

Spiro, R., & Collins, A. (1999). A tribute to Jan Hawkins. *The Journal of the Learning Sciences. 8*(3 & 4), 291–292.

Wertsch, J. V. (1995) The need for action in sociocultural research. In J. V. Wertsch, P. del Rio, & A. Alvarez (Eds.), *Sociocultural studies of mind* (pp. 56–74). New York: Cambridge University Press.

MIND, CULTURE, AND ACTIVITY, *10*(1), 9–25

Reflection at the Crossroads of Cultures

Xiaodong Lin

Teachers College
Columbia University

Daniel L. Schwartz

School of Education
Stanford University

This article explores how technologies can transform the obstacles of geographical and cultural distance into new opportunities for learning and personal growth. In particular, it focuses on the potential benefits of reflection in the context of cross-cultural exchange and how technology can bring those benefits to the classroom. Several instances of research explore the uses of technology for promoting cross-cultural contact as a way to expose students and teachers to fresh educational values and practices. A consistent result is that when people experience a new culture or community or even a new classroom, they report an increase in reflection about their identities, attributions, and responsibilities. Reflection appears as a deeply social act. Several examples highlight two social functions of reflection in the context of cross-cultural interaction. One function is to help people decide which aspects of culture to appropriate and how to adapt those aspects to their own interests. Another function is to help people become more receptive to the presence of different values and practices. The article conclude with a set of provisional design principles for encouraging learning through cross-cultural reflection.

Across cultures and histories, reflection is a valued mode of thought. For some, reflection is a mental technology for solving problems; for others, it is a thoughtful pause to reconsider the routines of life; and for still others, it is a disposition toward abstraction over impulse. Although the characterizations differ, there are family resemblances. Our research has explored the learning that results from technology-supported, cross-cultural interactions. Although it was not our initial focus, we have repeatedly found that reflection asserts itself. It appears with great force and mediates many of the benefits we might hope for. So much so, that it has led us to think of reflection as a deeply social act.

New views of education describe learning as the appropriation of cultural practices and the development of an identity within those practices (Boaler & Greeno, 2000; Holland, Lachicotte, Skinner, & Cain, 1998; Lave & Wenger, 1991; Wenger, 1998). We have asked people about their experiences entering new cultures, and they spontaneously mentioned the significance of reflection—reflection on their identities, their attributions, their abilities to communicate and learn, and even on their anxiety about whether they committed a faux pas earlier in the day. Yet, when we

Requests for reprints should be sent to Xiaodong Lin, Department of Mathematics, Science and Technology, Teachers College, Columbia University, 525 West 120th Street, Box 8, New York, NY 10027. E-mail: xlin@tc.columbia.edu

looked to the relevant educational literatures to learn more about reflection, for example, the literature on metacognition, we often found descriptions of what seemed more like careful moment-to-moment problem solving than deep reflection. This gap in the literature is problematic for any view of education that takes seriously the idea that learning involves engaging new cultural practices, whether in the extreme form of moving across continents and languages or in the subtle form of moving from one classroom to another. Reflection is a significant element of coming into contact with new cultural forms, and we believe it is worth understanding more fully. This article explores reflection at the crossroads of cultures, and it presents ways that technology can help.

The article is organized into four sections. The first section describes the social character of reflection and its common manifestation in cross-cultural interactions. The second section recounts educational goals for reflection and advocates a new approach that harnesses reflection rather than teaches it as a skill. The third section narrates our on-going application research that uses technology to support reflective cultural exchanges. The results have converged on two important applications of reflection when learning from a new culture. One is reflective adaptation by which people decide what aspects of a culture to appropriate and how to adapt those aspects to their interests. Without opportunities for reflective adaptation, people can become uncomprehending subordinates to practice or cynics stuck in ineffectual rejection. The second application is to promote reflective receptivity. For all but the most blatant social breakdowns, reflection requires that people recognize the possibility that there are specific alternatives to which they should attend. Given a routine life full of habitual beliefs, people are not always open to reflection. Interestingly, we have found that one of the important social functions of reflection is that when people see others reflecting, they become more receptive to reflecting on that person's point of view. In the concluding section, we summarize our research with six design principles for encouraging learning through reflection.

THE SOCIAL CHARACTER OF REFLECTION

Reflection, like deduction or imagery, is a specific manner of thought with its own character. Understanding that character can inform instructional decisions. In this section, we describe the social character of reflection.

By all accounts, reflection is concerned with developing a more coherent set of ideas and actions, and it should be distinguished from impulsive or routine behaviors. Because reflection often occurs in quiet moments, removed from the distractions of behavior, it is tempting to think of reflection as a solitary endeavor. The quiet nature of reflection, however, does not imply a non-social mode of thought as much as it indicates the intensity, vulnerability, and self-centeredness of reflection. Reflection is, after all, about ourselves and we can only expose ourselves and burden our friends so much.

One reason to view reflection as social is that it often takes the form of an internal dialog. Vygotsky and Piaget, for example, both proposed that internal reflection is an echo of external speech. Piaget (1967) wrote:

> Reflection is nothing other than internal deliberations, that is to say, a discussion, which is conducted with oneself just as it might be conducted with real interlocutors or opponents. One could then say that

reflection is internalized social discussion (just as thought itself presupposes internalized language). (p. 40)

A second reason to think of reflection as social, and the one we emphasize, is that its content is highly social. Piaget's emphasis on the abstract verbal nature of reflection misses this point. Thinking abstractly can occur without the emotional valence or questioning of assumptions that seems attached to self-reflection. As we report next, people who enter new cultures report an increase in reflection. We doubt this has to do with a sudden increase in their abilities for abstract thought; but instead, it has to do with heartfelt challenges to their identity and abilities to function.

Contact with new cultures is a significant catalyst to reflection, because reflection is often about one's relation to the social fabric. Calderhead (1989) described reflection "as a process of becoming aware of one's context, of the influence of societal and ideological constraints on previously taken-for-granted practices, and gaining control over the direction of these influences" (p. 44). Entering a new culture changes the social context and therefore one's relation to it, and this requires resorting goals, assumptions, and practices.

The significance of cultural contact for reflection can be illuminated by research relevant to the *contact hypothesis*, which was developed by social psychologists after World War II (see Hewstone & Brown, 1986). This basic hypothesis proposed that contact between members of different cultures would reduce prejudice. People would discover their similarities and thereby overcome their stereotypes. The hypothesis has had mixed success (Pettigrew, 1986). Contact does not guarantee an appreciation of similarities, and an appreciation of similarities does not guarantee the reduction of stereotypes and prejudice. Our approach is less ambitious. Instead of looking at how contact might lead to a hoped for distal consequence (i.e., prejudice reduction), we try to determine the proximal and dependable outcomes of cultural contact to see what educational goals they are likely to advance.

Based on our evidence, the proximal outcome of cultural contact, at least of a protracted and interactive sort, is reflection on one's identity. We interviewed 20 adults who had spent significant time participating in foreign cultures as students, workers, or spouses. We wanted to know if cross-cultural immersion would lead them to emphasize the discovery of similarities between peoples, or whether they would emphasize issues of identity and reflection in the face of manifest differences.

Among our various prompts, we asked for recurring insights and issues. Some people emphasized the language barrier that impeded understanding and participation in basic social interactions. They discovered that simply speaking the language did not mean they understood or were understood. Everyone spoke of challenges to their identity and their ability to function in a new setting. Across the responses, the depth of insight belied extended periods of reflection in which they reconsidered their identities vis-à-vis the differences between the prevailing culture and their origins. For example, a man who moved from China to the United States wrote:

> The identity issue. How can I be assimilated into the new culture without losing my own identity and how can I become and be perceived as a competent learner. Actually, I am more concerned about the identity issue in the latter sense: to rebuild my confidence of my own learning ability. I am not worrying much about losing my identity in the cultural sense. Even [if] there is something I need to change in order to be accepted into the new culture, I don't see this change in a negative sense as a loss. Rather I do think this is the reconciliation process I have to go through and there is price I have to pay for such

changes, especially at this beginning phase. Also I care much about in what way can I make the best use of my own culture in this new environment, and I think this combination of two cultures is the key to the successful survival in a new culture.

We asked if the interviewees would recommend that people spend extended periods of time in a foreign culture. Everyone said, "yes." This unanimous support might be due to our selection of people who had chosen to live abroad. Regardless, their reasons are informative. They uniformly said that it helped them learn something about who they are. For example, one woman thought she was not creative, until she lived in an environment where creativity was valued. Typically people said they learned something about themselves vis-à-vis their own culture. A woman who came from Greece to America stated:

> The main benefit of living and working in a new culture seems to be related to the fact that you gain experience of something new [compared] to the way you have been used to live. You become familiar with a different culture, which can ultimately lead you to make comparisons with your own culture. For me this proves to be a reason to eventually become more aware of your own identity.

Many people found they were representatives of the culture from which they came. An Asian-American woman who spent time in Hong Kong stated:

> I'm also viewed as an expert on the United States and responsible for its behavior—"Why do you let your children kill one another?" Naturally, I often fail to meet these expectations.

This led her to re-evaluate the way she made stereotypes and attributions about other people, as well as leading her to clarify her identity.

Notice that the path to reducing stereotypes was not to assume that other people are the same, but, rather, it was to learn that stereotypes mischaracterize the differences in other people's values and activities. For example, some found that they had a narrow conception of what constituted a good person. A schoolteacher believed that going to school and then college was a core social value when he first taught in an aboriginal culture. Over time he realized that the elders questioned the value of institutional schooling. He began to notice that for this culture school had led to frustration and failure without much economic benefit. He realized that level of schooling should not be the estimate of a person. As one woman who moved from the United States to Japan wrote:

> I don't know how or why, but people who have never lived in, or at least visited for longer periods of time, another culture advertise that fact with their very being. They lack an openness, and a level of human understanding—and they are not aware of it. I can only liken it to another level of experience such as becoming a parent.

Reflective experiences like these can be relevant to formal education. Students who come to America from Asia, often begin with the assumption that being an effective learner means memorizing well. When exposed to an environment that values questioning, these assumptions change, and the students become open to new paths of learning. Given that the proximal outcome of cross-cultural contact is reflection on one's identity and practices, it has led us to believe that we can set educational goals for the reflection that results from cross-cultural interaction.

THE GOALS OF REFLECTION

Teaching People to Be Reflective Versus Using Reflection to Improve Future Learning

Instruction that uses reflection has tended to emphasize the development of a reflective capacity. For example, Hatton and Smith (1995) claimed that "the end-point for fostering reflective approaches is the eventual development of a capacity to undertake reflection-in-action which is conceived of as the most demanding type of reflecting upon one's own practice" (p. 46). We do not subscribe to this use of reflection, particularly as it arises in cross-cultural settings. We use reflection to improve learning rather than to improve the skill to reflect per se. Nevertheless, instructing people to be more reflective has a powerful allure that spans both Western and Eastern traditions. One can appreciate this allure by noting how Western and Eastern philosophies identify functions of reflection that are taken up as goals within education.

In Western philosophy, the function of reflection is frequently associated with problem solving and explicit truth. A handbook on Western philosophy states:

> When thought, however, is bent on solving a problem, on finding out the meaning of a *perplexing* situation, or reaching a conclusion which is trustworthy, it is to be distinguished from other types of mental activity and should be called reflection. (Columbia Associates in Philosophy, 1923, p.2)

Reflection comprises justification and logical reasoning. Dewey (1933), for example, wrote:

> Reflection involves not only simply a sequence of ideas, but a consequence—a consecutive ordering in such a way that each determines the next as its proper outcome, while each outcome in turn leans back on, or refers to, its predecessors (p.4). [Reflection is the] active, persistent and careful consideration of any belief or supposed form of knowledge in light of the grounds that support it and the further conclusions to which it tends. (p. 9)

Metacognitive instruction adopts this function of reflection and attempts to teach it. Metacognition is the monitoring and regulating one's cognitive functioning (Brown, 1987; Flavell, 1979). In education, we teach students strategies of metacognition to help them order their thinking. By this view, we include reflection in our curriculum with the expectation that people will learn reflective skills to support future problem solving.

In Eastern philosophy, Confucius proposed that reflection achieves a balanced life. Confucius wrote:

> Self-reflection enhances your ability to conquer your own conflicts and weaknesses. It is the most important means to achieve a balanced mind within oneself. A balanced individual usually knows one's position in the community, is patient, is well mannered, and respects others and self. (Li, 1996, p.180)

According to Confucius, a society filled with balanced individuals will be peaceful and prosperous. Reflection is not reserved for problem solving, and the methods of reflection do not depend on checking one's reasoning. For example, reflection can occur at the end of each day through artistic expression. Reflection is a slow and habitual path to long-term enlightenment and harmony.

Japanese schools adapt these functions of reflection as goals of instruction. There are explicit periods to reflect on current activity, assess how it has gone, and question what school goals have been achieved today, this week, or this month (Sato, 1997). Reflection occurs orally or in writing; it can be cursory or lengthy; and it can be serious or somewhat trivial. Parents and teachers also participate in reflective activities with students on a routine basis. Such habits of mind are cultivated beginning in nursery schools (Lewis, 1995), and by the time students reach the sixth grade, they are often adept at the reflective habit, both as a self and group assessment processes. By this view, we include reflection in our curriculum to cultivate a reflective habit.

Limitations to teaching reflection.   Teaching people to be more reflective is a lofty goal and indicates reflection's social value. However, we question whether it is reasonable to suppose that a reflective turn of mind can be achieved within the confines of American courses that meet a few hours a week for a year. Like efforts to teach people logical reasoning (Nisbett, Fong, Lehman & Cheng, 1987), we suspect that the attempt to teach general skills of reflection may not fare well. People incline towards local knowledge over general skills. Reflection works best when it has specific issues to work through (e.g., Chi, DeLeeuw, Chiu, & LaVancher, 1994), and this requires knowing that something specific requires reflection, regardless of one's proficiency at reflection.

One way to see the importance of specificity for reflection is to notice that it is often retrospective. This is because people think best when they have a known specific context to work with (Gay & Cole, 1967), and reflection capitalizes on a specific past as opposed to a vague future. We offer a small and large example showing that reflection depends on specificity. The small example comes from a study that asked people to reflect on the accuracy of five astrological forecasts. Each individual in the study read one forecast per day. They were told that the forecasts applied to their sign (e.g., Gemini), though in reality they all had the same forecasts. One group of individuals read the forecasts over five mornings. Their job was to reflect on each forecast and rate, from 1 to 5, how applicable they thought it would be to their upcoming day. The other group read the forecasts in the evening. Their job was to rate how applicable the forecast had been for the just-ended day. The evening readers rated the applicability of the forecasts nearly 1.5 points higher than the morning readers did. The evening people could map the forecasts into a specific set of experiences, and therefore they had more ways to reflect on the forecasts' relevance. In contrast, the morning raters had little specific to reflect on, and, therefore, they could not as easily imagine ways the forecast would hold true.

The retrospective character of reflection indicates its dependence on specificity. This prerequisite of specificity becomes important when using reflection for educational goals. Simply telling people they should be reflective is like telling people they should think harder; it will not help people get very far unless they have something specific to think about. Noticing reflective opportunities can be very difficult. When embedded in the same situation day after day, people develop habitual ways of seeing. People can fail to reflect on key assumptions, even if they are willing to reflect and their reflection has been institutionalized as "a social practice in which all the participants are involved in modeling, using and making explicit their reflections" (Freese, 1999, p. 898). This point became exceedingly clear in a recent study with Chinese and American schools.

The study arose from a concern that metacognitive education pays attention to strategies but not to the goals that strategy training intends to achieve (Lin, 2001a). For example, students might not have learning as a primary goal, in which case no amount of skill training would help. The results of our study lend credence to this concern, but the results directly point to the difficulty of recognizing that a situation requires reflection.

We asked 281 fifth grade United States and Chinese students and their teachers to design an ideal student for their classes. The students and teachers came from either public or private schools (three classes were from each of the American and Chinese public schools, five classes were from an American private school, and four classes were from a Chinese private "key" school in China). The students and teachers generated five properties they thought were important for an ideal student. The properties generated naturally broke into three concerns: learning well, behaving well, and socializing well. Here, we only focus on learning and behaving. Properties that emphasized learning included "explaining ideas clearly," "being able to reason and think logically," "knowing when one makes mistakes," and so on. Properties for behaving included "not to fight in class," "sit still during the lecture," "follow classroom rules," and so on. To validate our ad hoc categories, we subsequently asked students what would happen if a boy did not do an assignment. Those students who emphasized learning tended to say, "The boy would not learn." Those students who emphasized behavior tended to say, "The boy would get in trouble."

Figure 1 presents the percentages of students and teachers from each nation and school type who mentioned learning and/or behavioral properties for their ideal students. Each group of students highly valued learning properties, except the American public school students. The American students listed behavioral properties instead. Significant for this discussion, the American public school teachers also emphasized behavior in their ideal students more than the other groups of teachers.

We showed these results to the American public school teachers. They were alarmed when they saw the ideals for their classrooms compared to the other schools. They had no idea that they and their students had been complicit in sustaining a classroom culture that valued behaving over learning. They immediately began to reflect on what they had been doing and how to change it. As is often the case, it is not what people worry about that gets them, it is what they don't.

Cross-cultural exposure can help illuminate specific issues that warrant reflection. In our instructional designs, we do not try to teach reflection. Instead, we orchestrate situations where re-

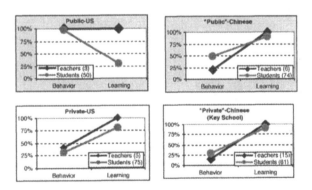

FIGURE 1   Percentage of students and teachers from United States and Chinese private and public schools who mentioned learning and/or behavioral properties for their ideal students.

flection naturally arises over specific issues that support the goal of helping people reflect on their educational identities and practices. The next section describes how we have used cross- cultural interactions with the aid of technology to foster two applications of reflection that are important to educational growth—adaptation and receptivity.

THE APPLICATION OF REFLECTION

Cross-cultural experiences generate excellent opportunities for reflection and learning. In addition to alternative models of practice, they provide contrasts that help people notice tacit elements of their own practice. It is important, however, to avoid the assumption that any cultural exposure leads to productive reflection. People can find a new culture repulsive. One American who lived in Ghana noted, "For some Americans, living in Africa was too much of a shock. I saw this happen. These Americans dismissed differences as pointing to others' inferiority. This kept them from learning about themselves." Culture can also be overwhelming. Durkheim (1951), for example, proposed two ways in which social structures can lead to suicide. With *anomie*, society does not provide sufficient direction for an individual to determine what constitutes a meaningful life. With *egoism*, society overly specifies the models of achievement, and people feel the pressure of falling short. Rousseau, whose *Social Contract* so influenced constitutional democracies, was ironically also an originator of existentialism. In *Reveries of the Solitary Walker,* Rousseau (1979) described how his culture rejected his uniqueness, and he was left to bitter reflections trying to rationalize a life without acceptance. Using cultural contact as a way to encourage learning is a double-edged sword.

When we design cross-cultural exchanges we need to protect our students and provide ways that they can adapt rather than simply adopt, reject, or flounder (e.g., Hammond, this issue). Technology can be a powerful ally. Not only does it enable cross-cultural exchanges, it allows people to meet new cultures in manageable pieces that target specific opportunities for reflection and subsequent changes to practice. Our approach has been to use technology so individuals can interact with another culture while remaining in their own. This technique protects them from the full force of another culture, and it encourages them to adapt their cross-cultural lessons into the life they have to lead right then and there.

Reflective Adaptation

Cultures meet through material artifact.   When educators speak of technology facilitating cultural exchange, they frequently mention communication technologies that enable people to talk or watch (e.g., Stigler & Heibert, 1999). Technology, however, is often the culture that gets exchanged. Anthropologists and cultural historians have documented the power of material artifacts in precipitating change, whether by innovations from within a culture (e.g., the printing press, Eisenstien, 1979) or by imported innovations (e.g., snowmobiles, Pelto & Muller-Wille, 1987). Surprisingly, there are few studies that examine this process in the context of classrooms. This seems like an important topic as we increasingly introduce technology into schools (Schofield, 1995).

Importing an artifact often involves importing cultural values and practices afforded by the artifact. If these values are in contrast to the local culture, they may lead to a process of reflection. In one study, we introduced an American educational artifact into a Hong Kong classroom (Lin, 2001b). Our method was consistent with a "breaching experiment" (Garfinkle, 1963). We hoped the artifact would disrupt normal practices so that tacit aspects of the classroom would become apparent to us. Although this happened, it occurred even more for the participants who became aware of their implicit practices and values.

This was a case study that documented how a fifth grade Hong Kong teacher used an educational artifact from the United States. After observing the teacher during a week of "routine" instruction, we asked her to spend a week using *The Adventures of Jasper Woodbury*, a video-based narrative that embodies American ideals about learning math in realistically complex, problem-solving contexts (Cognition and Technology Group at Vanderbilt, 1997). We interviewed the teacher and a sample of students throughout the process, and we videotaped and analyzed the daily lesson structure.

Figure 2 shows the instructional sequences for the four routine lessons and five Jasper lessons. The flow of the instruction was uniform for the routine lessons. When Jasper was introduced, the structure of the lessons shifted and became unpredictable from day to day. The artifact afforded different patterns of interaction and disrupted the previously regimented classroom. The students seized on the open-ended structure of Jasper. They rejected the teacher's attempts to follow the routine of an initial example followed by practice exercises and then assessment. Moreover, because a Jasper Adventure is complex, it typically takes a team effort. These students, who had not worked collaboratively, began to find they were extremely competitive. This raised challenges for the teacher and students to establish a new community of practice.

The challenges to the teacher's ability to sustain her regular classroom structure caused intense self-questioning. She worried that letting the students pursue their problem-solving inclinations would erode her authority in class, and she wondered whether letting students work together without her control meant she was no longer teaching. Ultimately, she made a series of justified decisions to adapt some of the affordances of Jasper and reject others. She adapted her role as teacher by providing lessons on a need-to-know basis instead of using "pre-instruction" at the start of each lesson. She let go of her desire to give in-class quizzes at the end of each day (perhaps not a good

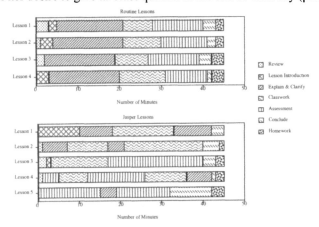

FIGURE 2   Daily instructional sequence for routine and Jasper lessons.

thing). Finally, she did not let students work through the problem at a completely independent pace, and she closely monitored their progress throughout the process of problem-solving.

The level of reflection was intense for the teacher as she began the transition from routine to adaptive expertise (Hatano & Inagaki, 1986). She had to make real decisions about whether to change her practices in response to the artifact and what those changes would mean for her identity. We have labeled this reflective adaptation. Unlike watching a videotape of a foreign classroom, the teacher could not treat this as an academic exercise in reflection. And unlike entering a new culture, she could not rely on the prevailing culture to determine the course of behavior. The level of responsibility was high as were the demands for agency—an ideal mix for productive reflection.

Instructional technologies for reflective adaptation.   Encouraging reflection via new technologies, like Jasper, can be powerful. But it is not always successful. One problem is that people may not be receptive to new technologies. The Hong Kong teacher was open to Jasper because she was in a school that was searching for ways to improve its standing in the community. Other Hong Kong schools rejected our overtures to introduce Jasper. Another problem is that many artifacts underspecify their use. In the movie, "The Gods Must Be Crazy," a soda bottle becomes a club. Although underspecification provides room for reflective adaptation, it can be a liability. Studies conducted within the United States showed that without guidance, teachers sometimes use Jasper in a way that disregards its potential for reform-based instruction. The artifact gets assimilated into the existing culture without causing much change in traditional teaching methods (Lin & Hatano, 2002). One way to address this challenge is to provide examples of practice to complement the technology. This is tricky because we want to provide guidance, but we do not want to imply there is only one way to use the artifact, which would undermine reflective adaptation.

In our designs of instructional technology, we try to encourage reflective adaptation. We offer teachers and students the responsibility and agency for adapting our technology to their needs, and we try to build in sufficient guidance so they see its educational potential. We originally called this *Flexibly Adaptive Instructional Design* (Schwartz, Lin, Brophy, & Bransford, 1999), but it might better be called *Reflectively Adaptive Instructional Design*.

As one instance, we created STAR.Legacy (Schwartz, Brophy, Lin, & Bransford, 1999). Legacy is a multimedia shell that embodies a set of practices for managing complex problem-, project-, and case-based activities. Figure 3 shows the software interface that suggests a sequence of events that are valuable for inquiry-based instruction. People click on the icons to reach "pages" that hold relevant activities. For example, the challenge icon brings students to a page that presents a problem or case they learn to solve using the rest of the inquiry cycle.

Legacy differs from instructional designs that expect teachers to comply with practices determined by remote instructional designers and which leave little opportunity for adaptation. Legacy offers practices and opportunities for reflection without overly prescribing the curriculum or sequence of activities. For any given instance of Legacy, there are activities and resources that we, as instructional designers, seed into the program. For example, in the domain of the life sciences, we built three progressive video challenges for understanding how exotic flora and fauna can affect an ecosystem, and we included a variety of supportive resources (e.g., anchor videos, expert commentary, web-links, self-assessment activities, simulations). More important, Legacy encourages students and teachers to add further content to adapt it to their local communities. For ex-

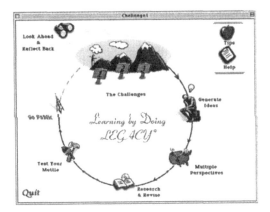

FIGURE 3   The STAR.Legacy, multimedia interface for supporting reflectively adaptive instructional design.

ample, students can interview community members who know something about plants and insects (e.g., at the garden store). They can then include these as resources, leaving a "legacy" for future generations of students. Similarly, teachers can incorporate new challenges, resources, and assessments that map into local curriculum standards. Ultimately, our goal is to have teachers and students adaptively reflect on what is important to learn and to capitalize on the strengths and needs of their local community (see Lee, this issue).

Reflective Receptivity

When immersed in another culture, people face personal challenges that cause them to reflect. When technology temporarily connects people who remain in their base cultures, there is less pressure to be reflective. People can draw on stereotypes rather than being receptive to reflection. To address this problem, we have taken the approach of "humanizing culture," which prior research shows can help people see past their stereotypes, at least temporarily (Macrae, Stangor, & Hewstone, 1996). As much as possible, we want to avoid anonymous cross-cultural contact. Instead of only presenting model practices by videotape or artifact, we help people develop an understanding for the individuals who use those practices and artifacts. This makes them more receptive to the values behind the practices and artifacts and leads to productive reflection.

Humanizing culture.   The value of humanizing culture appears in a study that compared presenting a "general culture" versus presenting an individual from a culture (Lin & Bransford, 2001). The study arose in the context of a growing concern about a disconnection between foreign professors and their American students. To explore possible solutions, we examined how "people knowledge" about a foreign professor would change student perceptions and inferences. The college students in the "Strange Professor" study began with a written case about Professor X from China who had difficulties with American college students. Students answered a number of questions about their perceptions of the problem and proposed solutions.

Following the baseline exercise, the students watched one of two videos. In one video, the participants saw a tour video that described the history, famous places, foods, and rituals of the professor's culture. In the other video, the participants heard the story of Professor X's challenges with political and social change as a child and coming to America. Afterward, members of each group were asked to answer questions about the case for a second time.

Prior to the videotapes, almost all of the participants saw the problem as Professor X and her unrealistic expectations. Afterwards, students who watched the tour video did not change their perceptions. One student wrote, "The professor is a typical Chinese who is rigid, critical, and boring." Another student wrote, "Like most Chinese, she is hard-working and values education, but is boring and strict and has few social skills." In contrast, students who watched the personal video altered their thinking. They integrated Professor X's cultural experiences into their thinking. One student wrote, "The professor realizes what life can be like without education because of the personal cultural experiences. She is a responsible professor, values education, and wants to provide her students with a good education."

To assess the degree to which these different experiences could support reflection, we asked the students from both conditions to rate the change in their understanding of the teacher's problem. Our assumption was that if they discerned a change, then they were in a better position to reflect on those changes. At the end of the study, students rated their level of understanding before and after the videotape on a scale of 1 to 5. Both groups of students rated their initial understanding at an average level of 2.1. However, the personal story students rated their subsequent understanding at 4.2, whereas the tour students felt their understanding merely increased to 2.4.

Although we did not test the students further, we suppose that the humanizing video gave them specific knowledge that would support reflection on their own beliefs and practices in regard to foreign teachers. General knowledge of a culture does not provide sufficient grist for the mill. On one level this is common sense—getting to know someone as an individual makes it harder to generalize and stereotype about that person. On another level, it significantly reinforces the value of integrating technology into the culture and reflection mix. Rather than being cold and depersonalizing, technology can be a catalyst to humanistic compassion.

Reflection humanizes oneself for others.   Reflection is a form of self-assessment. It is an attempt to re-evaluate one's actions and beliefs in light of the community in which one operates. Within schools, it is a good idea to encourage students to self-assess, if only for the reason that it engages students in thinking about their work more carefully. Self-assessment, however, can be difficult for the same reasons that reflection is difficult. It is hard to know what to assess, and it is hard to make assessments that go much beyond one's initial understanding. To promote self-assessment of student work as well as more profound reflections about themselves as learners, we have been asking students from different cultures to assess one another's homework via the Internet. A striking outcome from this work is that when people see evidence of other people being reflective, they become more receptive to those people and reflective themselves. This is one reason that we characterize reflection as a social act. Not only does it have social content for those who do the initial reflection, it also serves the social function of making other people more receptive.

In our first application of cross-cultural peer feedback, we asked middle school, social studies students from China to assess the homework of their counter parts in America. The homework was to write a story about a historical period of China. We quickly learned that this arrangement caused misunderstanding. The American students felt that the Hong Kong feedback was "too harsh," and they had little desire to revise their work in response. The Hong Kong students felt that they should be as critical as possible so the American students could learn more. To resolve this problem, we did not prescribe strategies for giving and receiving feedback because we knew our rules could not cover all the misunderstandings that might arise. Instead, we tried to humanize the activity so the students would naturally become more receptive to one another's values.

To humanize the exchange, the American students sent their stories along with self-assessments of those stories. The American students wrote how well they had created stories that had main ideas, were interesting, and were accurate. They also wrote of any difficulties in doing the assignment. Our thought was that including the students' self-assessments and reflections would cause the Hong Kong students to comment not only about the student artifacts but also about the students who produced them. They would become receptive to the needs of the American students causing them to be more reflective about their role vis-à-vis the American students.

Half of the Hong Kong students read the stories plus self-assessments, and the other half only read the stories. The Hong Kong students worked in groups to provide written feedback to the students. The Hong Kong students who did not see the self-assessments were uniformly critical in their feedback. The Hong Kong students who saw the self-assessments were more positive and encouraging. One group of Hong Kong students wrote:

> Your story was not very deep and complex. You should also write about life of upper class people of the time rather than only about lower class people because you need to provide a complete picture of the life in that time. However, from your self-assessment, we felt that you are willing to look into yourself for improvement and you are quite thorough about it. Overall, you guys seem to be good people.

The submissions that included self-assessments elicited friendlier and more specific feedback about possible improvements. Interview data showed that American students who received the more receptive feedback felt more of a bond with the Hong Kong students and indicated more willingness to continue working with them. They tended to view the suggestions for revisions positively rather than as a sign of failure.

The American self-assessors also began to reflect on themselves as learners relative to the values exhibited in the Hong Kong feedback. They noticed important learner characteristics exemplified by the Hong Kong students, including clear and logical explanations and a serious attitude toward schoolwork. They also found that the Hong Kong students' English grammar was only average, which might open an avenue for reciprocity.

Overall, signs of reflection and self-assessment in others made members of both cultures more receptive to thinking about one another's beliefs, practices, and artifacts. As fits our general story, reflection is valued, at least across these cultures, and seeing others reflect causes people to be more compassionate, receptive, and ultimately more reflective.

CONCLUSION

Summary

Learning often involves developing new identities and activities within a cultural matrix, and we have argued that reflection is a signature quality of this development. We find that when people move to a new culture or community, or even a new classroom, they report an increase in reflection about their identities, goals, and responsibilities in relation to the values of the old and new communities. The goal of this article has been to initiate a discussion on the potential benefits and conditions of productive reflection when people meet new cultures and how we can bring those benefits to the classroom. Much of our research has explored the uses of technology for promoting cross-cultural contact. It can expose students and teachers to fresh models of educational values and practices, and can illuminate their own. In this context, the value of reflection for most people is not simply to be more reflective. Instead, they try to learn a specific body of knowledge about themselves and the cultural basis for their beliefs, and ideally this knowledge can guide their future actions.

An important function of reflection is to help people decide which aspects of a new culture to appropriate and how to adapt those aspects to their own interests. But, for reflection to take place, people must notice and be receptive to other points of view and activities. To achieve reflective adaptation and receptivity, we believe that students and teachers must take on responsible roles that require authentic decisions. Being a tourist is not always sufficient to make people either receptive or sincerely reflective. Technology is useful in this regard because it enables manageable cross-cultural exchanges that target specific learning goals for reflection. At the same time, technology allows people to interact with a foreign culture while maintaining responsibility to their local culture.

Design Principles for Fostering Productive Reflection

We have been working toward principles that can help design productive environments for reflective learning through cross-cultural exchange. There are many possible principles. We highlight those principles that are derived from the preceding discussion.

1. Create reflective activities that target educational goals.
2. Include opportunities for responsible action that motivate genuine reflection.
3. Present culture in bite-sized pieces, which help focus reflection, and are sufficiently manageable that individuals can affect changes based on their reflections.
4. Encourage solitary reflections that may be communicated.
5. Design technology that suggests practices but encourages adaptation.
6. Humanize cultural contact so people will be receptive to reflection.

A Summary Example that Incorporates the Six Design Principles

We conclude with a recent Internet intervention that highlights the six design principles. With Jeff Holmes, we designed a virtual learning space (VLS) in which we asked a teacher in Hong Kong whom we will call Sally, and a teacher in the United States, Cindy, to teach a group of students a biology lesson. The teachers never met each other or their students face-to-face. Instead, they conducted class in a web-based, virtual reality where they appeared to one another as avatars and communicated in real-time by typing. Figure 4 provides a summary of the activities the teachers completed and a glimpse of the VLS that we built.

To foster reflective activities that target learning goals (Principle 1), we created an experiment on insect habitats in the VLS. By co-planning and co-teaching around the experiment, we hoped the cross-cultural interactions would help the teachers increase their content knowledge, pedagogical skills, and appreciation of different learning goals.

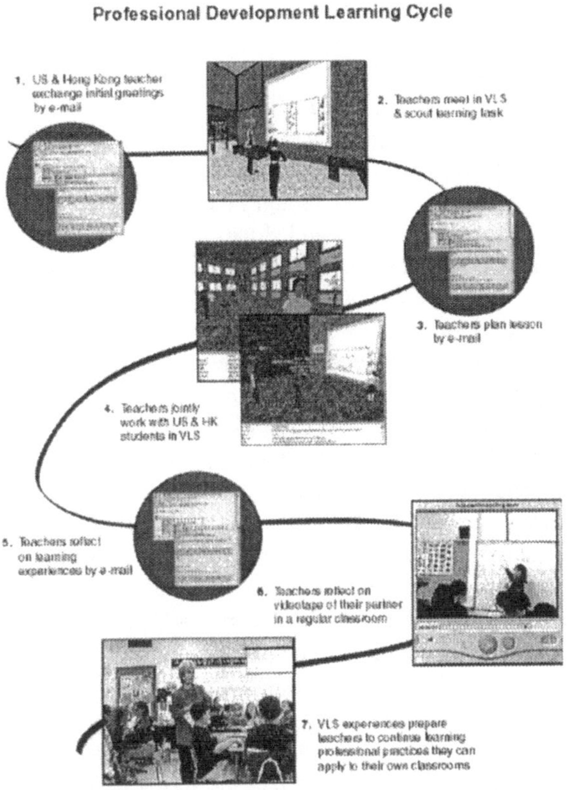

Professional Development Learning Cycle

FIGURE 4   The sequence of teacher activities as they prepared and met with students in a virtual learning space.

To enhance authentic responsibility (Principle 2), teachers had the joint agency of teaching real children in real time. They had to make decisions about whether to change their normal practices in response to the VLS and what those changes would mean to them and their students.

To permit adaptive changes, the teachers interacted with another culture while remaining in their own (Principle 3). This protected teachers from the full force of another culture and allowed them to reflectively adapt their cross-cultural peer's values and practices into their on-line teaching.

To allow moments for reflection (Principle 4), we asked teachers to plan their lesson through e-mail before they started teaching. The solitary opportunities to reflect on what they would say in their e-mails gave the teachers a chance to consider and craft their thoughts. During the planning, they spontaneously wrote what was important to each of them and how to compromise in areas of disagreement. This reflection, when made social, enabled the teachers to learn about one another's strengths and their own weaknesses. Cindy e-mailed the Hong Kong teacher, "I am so impressed with you! You have such a command of the science experiment design that I think you ought to be teacher A, who teaches content and I can be teacher B (the social one) and whisper with you and encourage talk among the students. Fondly, Cindy." Meanwhile, Sally learned about Cindy's talents for creating a supportive atmosphere for student learning. These early exchanges were important once the teachers actually met the students and had to make on-the-spot decisions. When they had trouble controlling the students, Sally asked Cindy to take charge, but when a question arose about the experimental logic, Cindy asked Sally to take over.

To suggest practices while encouraging adaptation (Principle 5), we designed a web-based experiment on insect habitats that highlighted variable control. This afforded specific practices for the students and teachers. At the same time, we under specified the goal of the lesson. We simply asked them to teach the students what they thought the students should learn. This invited each teacher to project and revise her own goals and values during the lesson preparation.

To humanize the cultural contact (Principle 6), we asked the teachers to exchange e-mails to prepare their lesson. The multiple exchanges helped each teacher reflect on the human values behind the other's instructional preferences. These interactions led to the formation of personal bonds as revealed by the content and frequency of their e-mails (19 e-mails during the week of planning, and three per week for 6 months after).

By our account, the VLS experience should have influenced the teacher's receptiveness to one another's knowledge and practice. To examine this hypothesis, we collected videotapes of Sally and Cindy working in their regular classroom. We asked uninvolved (non-VLS) teachers to observe the videotapes and notice any valuable lessons for themselves, just as they might do in a professional development setting. These control teachers tended to dismiss any novel practices they noticed. For example, the control teachers from the United States claimed that the high structure and intellectual discipline of the Hong Kong classroom could never be accomplished in America. In contrast, the VLS teachers did not relegate differences to "culture," and they considered ways to adapt some of the shown practices and values into their own culture. For example, the American teacher saw the high expectations of the Hong Kong teacher had for her students, which caused her to reflect on whether she had allowed her expectations and standards to sink too low.

Ultimately, we will need more work to explain the forms of knowledge that emerge at the crossroad of cultures with the support of technology, and we need more understanding of how to use technology as a catalyst to reflection. Ideally, we will form design principles so technologies can transform the obstacles of geographical and cultural distance into new opportunities for learning, compassion, and personal growth. This, we believe, is the legacy of Jan Hawkins.

ACKNOWLEDGMENTS

The writing of this article, and much of the reported research, has been supported by the Spencer Foundation. The opinions expressed in the article are those of the authors and not the foundation.

REFERENCES

Boaler, J., & Greeno, J. G. (2000). Identity, agency, and knowing in mathematics worlds. In J. Boaler (Ed.), *Multiple perspectives on mathematics teaching and learning*. Stamford, CT: Elsevier Science.

Brown, A. L. (1987). Metacognition, executive control, self- regulation and other more mysterious mechanisms. In F. E. Weinert, & R. H. Kluwe (Eds.), *Metacognition, motivation, and understanding* (pp. 65–116): Hillsdale, NJ: Lawrence Erlbaum Associates, Inc.

Calderhead, J. (1989). Reflective teaching and teacher education. *Teaching & Teacher Education, 5,* 43–51.

Chi, M. T., DeLeeuw, N., Chiu, M. H., & LaVancher, C. (1994). Eliciting self-explanations improves understanding. *Cognitive Science, 18,* 439–477.

Cognition and Technology Group at Vanderbilt (1997). *The Jasper project: Lessons in curriculum, instruction, assessment, and professional development.* Mahwah, NJ: Lawrence Erlbaum Associates, Inc.

Columbia Associates in Philosophy (1923). *An introduction to reflective thinking.* New York: Houghton Mifflin.

Dewey, J. (1933). *How we think.* Boston: Heath.

Durkheim, E. (1951). *Suicide.* New York: Free Press.

Eisenstein, E. L. (1979). *The printing press as an agent of change: Communications and cultural transformations in early modern Europe.* New York: Cambridge University Press.

Flavell, J. H. (1979). Metacognition and cognitive monitoring: A new area of cognitive-developmental inquiry. *American Psychologist, 34,* 906–911.

Freese, A. R. (1999). The role of reflection on pre-service teachers' development in the context of a professional development school. *Teaching & Teacher Education, 15,* 895–909.

Garfinkel, H. (1963). A conception of, and experiments with, "trust" as a condition of stable concerted actions. In O. J. Harvey (Ed.), *Motivation and social interaction* (pp. 187–238). New York: Ronald.

Gay, J., & Cole, M. (1967). *The new mathematics and an old culture; a study of learning among the Kpelle of Liberia.* New York: Holt, Rinehart, & Winston.

Hatano, G., & Inagaki, K. (1986). Two courses of expertise. In H. A. H. Stevenson & K. Hakuta (Eds.), *Child development and education in Japan* (pp. 262–272). New York: Freeman.

Hatton, N., & Smith, D. (1995). Reflection in teacher education: Towards definition and implementation. *Teaching & Teacher Education, 11,* 33–49.

Hewstone, M., & Brown, R. (1986). Contact is not enough: An inter-group perspective on the 'Contact Hypothesis.' In M. Hewstone & R. J. Brown (Eds.), *Contact and conflict in inter-group encounters* (pp. 1–44). Oxford, England: Blackwell.

Holland, D., Lachicotte, W., Skinner, D., & Cain, C. (1998). *Identity and agency in cultural worlds.* Cambridge, MA: Harvard University Press.

Lave, J., & Wenger, E. (1991). *Situated learning: Legitimate peripheral participation.* New York: Cambridge University Press.

Lewis, C. C. (1995). *Educating hearts and minds.* New York: Cambridge University Press.

Li, D. Y. (1996). *The wisdom and philosophy of Confucius.* SiZuan, China: Educational.

Lin, X. D. (2001a). Designing metacognitive activities. *Educational Technology Research & Development, 49*(2), 23–40

Lin, X. D. (2001b). Reflective adaptation of a technology artifact: A case study of classroom change. *Cognition & Instruction, 19,* 395–440.

Lin, X. D., & Bransford, J. D. (2001). *People knowledge: A missing ingredient in many of our educational designs.* Unpublished manuscript, Vanderbilt University, Nashville, TN.

Lin, X. D., & Hatano, G. (2002). Cross-cultural adaptation of educational technology. In T. Koschmann, R. Hall, & N. Miyake (Eds.), *CSCL2: Carrying Forward the Conversation* (pp. 89–97). Hillsdale, NJ: Lawrence Erlbaum Associates, Inc.

Macrae, C. N., Stangor, C., & Hewstone, M. (Eds.). (1996). *Stereotypes and stereotyping.* New York: Guilford.

Nisbett, R. E., Fong, G. T., Lehman, D. R., & Cheng, P. W. (1987). Teaching reasoning. *Science, 238,* 625–631.

Pelto, P. J., & Muller-Wille, L. (1987). Snowmobiles: Technological revolution in the Arctic. In H. R. Bernard & P. J. Pelto (Eds.), *Technology and social change* (pp. 207–258). Prospect Heights, IL: Waveland.

Pettigrew, T. F. (1986). The inter-group contact hypothesis reconsidered. In M. Hewstone & R. J. Brown (Eds.), *Contact and conflict in inter-group encounters* (pp. 169–195). Oxford, England: Blackwell.

Piaget, J. (1967). *Six psychological studies* (A. Tenzer, Trans.; Elkind, Ed.) New York: Random House.

Rousseau, J. J. (1979). *The reveries of the solitary walker.* (C.E. Butterworth, Trans.) New York: New York University Press.

Sato, N. E. (1997). *Forms and functions of reflection in Japanese elementary schools.* Paper presented at American Educational Research Association, Chicago, IL.

Schofield, J. W. (1995). *Computers and classroom culture.* Cambridge, England: Cambridge University Press.

Schwartz, D.L., Brophy, S., Lin, X. D., & Bransford, J. D. (1999). Software for managing complex learning: Examples from an educational psychology course. *Educational Technology Research & Development, 47*(2), 39–59.

Schwartz, D., Lin, X. D., Brophy, S., & Bransford, J. D. (1999). Toward the development of flexibly adaptive instructional designs. In C. M. Reigeluth (Ed.), *Instructional design theories and models: A new paradigm of instructional theory* (pp. 183–214). Mahwah, NJ: Lawrence Erlbaum Associates, Inc.

Stigler, J., & Hiebert, J. (1999). *The teaching gap: Best ideas from the world's teachers for improving education in the classroom.* New York: Free Press.

Wenger, E. (1998). *Communities of practice: Learning, meaning, and identity.* Cambridge, England: Cambridge University Press.

MIND. CULTURE, AND ACTIVITY, *10*(1), 26–41

Building Houses, Building Lives

Lorie A. Hammond

Department of Teacher Education
California State University at Sacramento

This article uses a narrative format to describe situations in which immigrant families from a Southeast Asian hill tribe, the Mienh, adapt to technological and cultural change within a California elementary school which sponsors a family literacy, school–community garden, and house building project. Much has been written about the ways in which immigrant families and personnel at their schools struggle to communicate. My thesis is that even in the case of immigrants experiencing huge cultural and technological change, from an oral subsistence culture to an urban technological society, adjustments can be creative and empowering, if schools incorporate community "funds of knowledge" into their instructional plan. Real projects such as storytelling, gardening, and house building provide rich contexts for intercultural dialogues which enable teachers and Mienh parents to build a *Mienh-American house*, a symbolic construct in which both traditional and modern technologies are combined.

The social world is a world in becoming, not a world in being. (Turner, 1974, p. 24)

In this issue, we build on the work of Jan Hawkins, a work which explores the connections between human development, technology, and cultural diversity. My particular interest is in the dynamics which occur when people learn each others' technologies, in intercultural contexts where old and new, Eastern and Western cultures interact in meaningful educational settings. In particular, I am interested in encouraging and studying those rare settings where both traditional and modern knowledge are integrated and valued. I am also interested in how people who experience rapid technological change, from subsistence villages to modern cities, within and without national borders, make sense of the world around them. How do they make decisions about what to do in their day-to-day lives? And, how do these decisions reflect cultural conflict, resolution and transformation?

This study focuses on members of the Mienh hill tribe, a minority group from the remote mountains of Laos, Thailand, and Vietnam, who were displaced in large numbers in the 1970's and 1980's by the War in Vietnam and its extensions. A group of several hundred Mienh people settled in our low income California urban area about 10 years ago, joining a large, diverse community of other immigrants, refugees, and transient Americans. Whereas the adjustment of all refugee children and their families to mainstream American schools is challenging, the Mienh face an extreme set of challenges as a group which (a) is small in number world-wide; (b) shares an oral rather than a written culture; and (c) has subsisted through slash and burn agriculture, hunting, and gathering. There is great contrast between the knowledge and technologies shared within the

---

Requests for reprints should be sent to Lorie A. Hammond, Department of Teacher Education, California State University at Sacramento, 6000 J Street, Sacramento, CA 95819–6079. E-mail: lhammond@csus.edu

Mienh culture and those assumed in a modern school, a fact which can lead to cultural conflict and makes the interaction between teachers and families particularly fascinating to study.

This article emerged from an unusual opportunity: that of working with a group of Mienh immigrants for several years on a family literacy and school–community garden and house building project, and of traveling to Thailand with a refugee woman, Liew, as she reunited with her family there. The family literacy and school garden project was an intentional intervention based on an attempt to integrate community "funds of knowledge" (Moll & Gonzalez, 1992) into the school instructional plan, in an attempt to balance the unequal power dynamic which usually occurs when an oral culture confronts a modern, written one (Goody, 1987). In this project, mainstream teachers and Southeast Asian parents collaborated with children to build a garden and field house at an urban California school, and to write stories about their work. This project not only enabled the teaching of science, literacy, technology (including computers), and multicultural education to school children and their families. It also transformed a mainstream school into an intercultural laboratory where teachers, parents, and children from different backgrounds were forced to communicate and resolve differences as they worked together toward common goals. It is the thesis of this article that immigrants' adjustment to technical and cultural change can be complex, creative, and empowering, rather than linear, reactive, and oppressive. Much depends on the ways in which institutions, such as schools, react to those they serve.

THEORETICAL UNDERPINNINGS

The three words whose relationship we were asked to ponder in this issue are technology, multicultural education, and human development. I am approaching this task through a single case—of one immigrant group in one urban school—as an example of a broader problem. This article is based on empirical observations which might be thought of as "notes from the field." Its theoretical frame is derived from current explorations in anthropology, and in multicultural and science education. My hope is to create a series of *caselets* (Arrellano et al., 2000) or short narratives, which illustrate how broad ideas such as multiple-perspectives take on palpable meaning in situations where people from different backgrounds struggle to solve problems together.

The word *technology,* a familiar term in anthropology, where it may refer to anything from language to an arrow to an atomic bomb, is most used in current popular press and educational circles to refer to computer related endeavors. Although computers were one tool used in the storytelling aspect of this project—and although the use of computers provides an exciting leap for previously nonliterate refugee families—my focus is on technology in the broadest of senses. Webster (2002) defines *technology* as "the science or study of the practical or industrial arts." The word traces from the Greek *techne,* which means art, and *logos,* which means discourse. In other words, discourse about the human arts. In my case, the focus will be on the arts and techniques which people apply in their daily lives: on what they eat, wear, and buy, and on how they grow their food and build their houses. Since people's use of technology reflects choices and therefore values, people's patterns of adaptation, resistance, and transformation within the possibilities they encounter, are indicators of cultural development. Most valuable are situations in which people discuss the choices they make, and why they make them. Intercultural projects necessitate and create rich opportunities for dialogue.

The Link to Multiculturalism

How do people's technological decisions relate to multiculturalism? Much has been written in multicultural education about the disproportionate school failure which occurs within minority groups when they are forced to assimilate to mainstream schools, which do not recognize or incorporate their own language and culture (Boggs, with Watson-Gegco & McMillen, 1985; Heath, 1983; Philips, 1983; Sleeter & Grant,1988). Yet neither the idea of tradition maintenance, through the preservation of culture and language in new settings, nor the idea of assimilation, through taking on American ways, adequately cover the complex adjustments which immigrants—and others—make on a daily basis in a constantly evolving modern world.

Studies of immigration, including the Suarez-Orozcos's (2001) recent work, reveal ways in which current trends in immigration differ from those which occurred at the turn of the 20th century, the time period most parallel to the 1990's in the numbers of immigrants entering the United States, and from which we draw many of our expectations about immigrant adjustment. The immigration experience of 1900–1910 involved people from Southern and Eastern Europe, as well as Ireland, who flooded America's cities (Suarez-Orozcos, 2001). These immigrants were European, although often poor and uneducated, and the world they entered was an industrial one. They made their way in factories and sweat-shops, following a now-familiar trajectory of gradual success through hard work and assimilation over several generations. By contrast, today's immigrants are generally from the developing world, from Asia and Latin America in the case of California, and the economy they enter is post-industrial, with fewer jobs for unskilled laborers, yet greater flexibility. The trajectory of success for immigrant groups is much more variable than that of their ancestors, depending on their education level, their country of origin, and their quickness to adapt. There are dramatic successes and dramatic failures, both between and within groups, and education plays a major role in both.

The Links Between Immigration, Globalization, and Human Development

Another striking aspect of immigrant adjustment today is the mobility of people worldwide, in an increasingly global economy, and the parallel if disproportionate development of all levels of education, wealth, and technology within most countries. Vietnamese film maker Trinh T. Minh stated that "there is a third world in every first world and vice versa." (quoted in Lippard, 1990, p. 18) Indeed, an elite in most developing nations enjoys similar privileges and shares many cultural attributes with the elite within the United States and other first world nations; while there are pockets in first world cities where poverty, access to technology, and cultural patterns resemble those of the third world. Such pockets tend to house diverse groups of native urban poor, combined with various immigrant groups. In these places, cultural contrasts reach dynamic proportions. For example, in my community of study, one shopping center houses an American discount supermarket, Russian delicatessen which also sells car insurance, Mienh grocery, Latin American astrologer, Western saddle shop, Mongolian barbecue, Chinese dim sum stand, pizza parlor, and taqueria. The clients of this shopping center are a combination of immigrants from many parts of the world and of poor urban Americans, whose families immigrated many decades ago, including homeless people, prostitutes, and drug dealers.

Near this shopping center there are several blocks of sprawling low cost apartment complexes which have housed a thousand or more Southeast Asian refugees for the past 10 years. More Common, immigrant families live in these complexes for several years before finding other housing. The apartments are run-down and rat-infested, a third world within a first world. Yet life there re-enacts rich patterns from the residents' countries of origin. Fish from the river and vegetables grown in vacant lots are sold from ice chests in the trunks of cars. Old women wearing Mienh turbans, or Hmong hats and traditional costumes, squat on bamboo stools as they chat and embroider in the California sunshine. Children are everywhere, in blue jeans, T-shirts, and tennis shoes, leading babies who wear traditional bonnets elaborately embroidered by their grandmothers.

Similarly, in Thailand, forces of modernization and globalization are transforming the lives of *fourth world* people, defined as those groups who have historically participated little in the cash economy, in the politics of any nation, or in formal schooling. For Mienh people, and others like them throughout the world, the lure of modernization, coupled with pressures placed on their agricultural traditions, by global markets and struggles over land use, are creating rapid change. For some, this change represents the opportunity to get educated and participate successfully in the world economy. For many others, economic independence as self-sufficient rural farmers is being replaced by economic dependence as poor, urban wage earners. Although this transition introduces more cash into people's lives than before, the contrast between a noncash economy where people produce everything they need and a cash economy where many people become too "poor" to meet their needs (to say nothing of their newly acquired wants), is a sobering one, which points out the relative nature of poverty in all countries.

In both the United States and Thailand, Mienh people are being forced into a multicultural life style in which they must cross cultural boundaries to carry out their daily lives. These adjustments are dramatic for a group that had isolated itself for hundreds of years to avoid participation in modernization and change. For example, neither Liew, my informant, nor any of her siblings, attended school when they grew up in Thailand, yet all of their children now attend schools in Thailand or the United States. In both countries, their children's schooling is in a second language and a foreign cultural setting. How do parents like Liew and her sisters relate to their children's schooling?

Goody (1987) described the transition between oral and written cultures all over the world, made more intense by the introduction of schools.

> With compulsory schooling there is an increasing tendency ... to see proper knowledge as coming from books alone; it is they that tell the truth, not the knowledge we obtain from our parents (i.e., the elders) or from our peers, nor yet directly from nature itself. (p. 163)

The Mienh are at the point of transition from oral to written culture, in both the United States and Thailand. Goody points out that in traditional cultures, there are generally three ways of obtaining knowledge. They are (a) basic knowledge, learned through sharing the experience of practical things like gardening and building; (b) "deep" cultural and spiritual knowledge codified in traditional ceremonies led by elders; and (c) knowledge which comes directly to individuals from the spiritual and natural world. These three ways of learning are all prominent in Mienh culture, in which people value practical knowledge, the knowledge of shamans, and their personal experiences with nature and with the ever-present spiritual world. School knowledge is different from these forms of knowledge, and tends to devalue the skills, wisdom, and spirituality of traditional people. The garden and house building, as well as bookmaking, projects described below are all aimed at a vision of human development which is multicultural, and builds on previous languages and cultures, rather than discrediting them in the face of current knowledge. In addition, it is the premise of our project that real-life activities, such as gardening and house building, help children from any background to create understandings about the natural world and the human technologies upon which literacy and academic discourse can be built.

The focus of this article is on the intercultural activities and dialogues, which evolved when two very different cultures worked together. "Intercultural" spaces are different than "cross-cultural" ones, as Lippard (1990) explained:

> Intercultural, suggesting a back and forth motion, might be an improvement on cross-cultural, which implies a certain finality—a cross-over or one way trip from margins to center, from lower to middle class, rather than a flexible exchange. (p. 17)

What is appealing about Lippard's definition is the notion of exchange, the lack of that linear sense of "progress" so typical of educational efforts which attempt to "help" immigrants to adjust to a static notion of mainstream life, or, in an equally limited fashion, to remain fixed in their own traditions. The stories below describe such two-way interactions.

METHODOLOGY

My research method is narrative. Clandinin and Connelly (2000) suggested that narrative inquirers "make themselves as aware as possible of the many, layered narratives at work in their inquiry space" (p. 70). These layered narratives occur in three dimensions: place (situation), time (past, present, and future), and interaction (personal and social; Clandinin & Connelly, 2000).

In this project, each dimension takes on complex meaning and applies to a variety of situations. The definition of place or situation includes not only the intercultural space created by the garden, but also the technological context in which our work is done. Hence, the place in which this building project occurred represents the interface between, not only home, and school, but also Western and Eastern, subsistence and modern ideas. Similarly, the notion of time has several meanings in the context of this project. Mienh elders represent an important time relationship within Mienh culture: the wisdom of elder versus younger men. This continuum was very important both to the elders and to the young Asian teachers involved, yet was invisible to mainstream teachers, who are unaccustomed to Mienh age-related hierarchies. In addition, there was the time dimension of the project itself. Mienh fathers wanted to build the garden house as quickly as possible, as they would in their villages, when people would travel to help each other build a house over an intense, 2-day period. Yet the time frame of the school demanded that the house only be built between 8:00 a.m.–2:00 p.m. each day, so that schoolchildren from both Mienh and other groups could participate. Finally, there is the time dimension of past, present, and future within participants' culturally organized lives. For example, Mienh parents at first insisted that the roof of the house be made of palm leaves, then agreed on metal. They justified this change on the grounds that in Thailand, people near the cities now use metal roofs. Their decision demonstrates how Mienh people define their own cultural identities in the United States in relation to the changing face of Asia.

The third dimension of narrative research is the one on which we will focus most: the interpersonal dimension. It is my premise that when people work together toward a common purpose, they are motivated to overcome cultural differences which they would never confront in a less "real" situation which did not demand resolution. Building a house, planting a garden, or cooking a meal—along with storytelling and other art forms—are cultural activities in which technology and resources interact with traditions and values of all the participants. As noted earlier, in such authentic activities, previously invisible cultural patterns emerge, creating opportunities for misunderstanding and conflict and/or for the building of new intercultural understandings on the part of all players.

This article chronicles 5 years of work, initially through a family literacy project, which evolved into a garden and house building project. A major purpose of these projects was to reverse the usual status relationship between oral and written cultures, as defined by Goody above, by enabling traditional cultural practices to become part of the school instructional plan. Various technologies, from computers to tape recorders to bamboo craft, became the tools through which these cultural practices were represented and recorded. Simultaneously, these tools and products became the record through which the intercultural journey can be recorded and analyzed.

CASE # 1: A TWO-WAY FAMILY LITERACY PROJECT

San Chow the Shaman sat at a school table, converted to an altar, rhythmically chanting and reading from a parchment book with painted Chinese characters. On the altar sat a recently sacrificed chicken, a pot of burning incense, small glasses of wine, and a large pile of spirit paper soon to be ignited and sent as an offering to the spirit world. San Chow was negotiating with the spirits of his ancestors about whether the new family literacy project, which opened that day, should become a center for Mienh people. He communicated with spirits by throwing carved bamboo pieces, which would indicate, depending on how they land, their answer to San Chow's queries. Bamboo has a wise spirit, our translator explains, because it is old and self- sustaining. It is a spirit whose advice we should seek.

San Chow was testing the water for his people, who knew they needed to learn English and job skills, but were not sure whether to trust the new English literacy center which had opened in their apartment complex. His first test was to see whether the center coordinator would allow him to hold a ceremony in which he asked for their ancestors' consent. This family literacy center was coordinated by a Peace Corps-trained teacher who knew that to attract a group of adult students already traumatized by war, internment, and immigration, she needed to create a place where they could build new skills within a familiar cultural complex. The ceremony was held in an apartment complex where Southeast Asian families lived, and was not subject to the social boundaries, such as the separation between church and state, which apply to schools and other public institutions. The spirits agreed to Mienh participation in the center on certain conditions, such as hiring their Shaman as childcare provider.

The family literacy project developed into a center where parents and children could use the communication of their own experiences as the basis for English practice. Even subjects like science were taught as cultural exchanges about how the world works. It was from such discussion that the garden project developed as a way to enhance community food security and explore connections between ethnobotany and Western science. A major activity that developed at the Center was the recording of traditional stories in the form of illustrated books to be shared with school classrooms. Mienh people had no secular written language in Thailand, although, their shamen write sacred documents in an ancient dialect of Chinese. Hence, historical traditions and morality tales were traditionally passed on through stories, which were told for hours each evening around the fire. Families involved in the literacy project were very aware that these unrecorded stories are in danger of being lost now that Mienh people watch television and work outside the home rather than spending their evenings telling stories. They therefore took great interest in recording their folk tales and accounts of daily life on computers at the literacy project.

Recording Traditional Stories in Print

The recording of stories from an oral tradition onto computers and then into printed books raises many questions about the relationship between technology and content. How different is a story expressed in printed type from the same story told by an elder in a fire-lit room? How much of the message is the story itself, how much the experience of storytelling? Goody (1987) asserted that when the written word becomes inserted in an oral culture, profound changes occur: (a) The actor, moving from storyteller to writer, becomes separated from the audience. (b) Knowledge becomes set in type, and can be passed without being reinterpreted through the lens of the storyteller. (c) Doctrines and ideologies are formed, which can then be juxtaposed with each other. In short, "the opposition between 'learned,' for example, booklearned and 'unlearned', for example, un-schooled,... divides the whole society and the whole culture" (p. 161). According to Goody, this division is between those who have access to literacy, and those who do not. In the current school context, this divide takes several forms. Parents, receiving literacy training, and grandparents, with no literacy, come to be seen as less competent than young children who quickly become fluent in English and in reading. This reverses the power hierarchy in Mienh families, where elders are most revered. In addition, the "digital divide" and other privileges separate school children in poor communities from more affluent children with home access to new technologies and other resources.

Although we are concerned about the ways in which literacy changes Mienh culture, we are also excited about the possibility of incorporating Mienh stories into the school instructional plan, thus reversing the typical power relation which Goody (1987) described between oral and written cultural groups. Mienh and other immigrant families are empowered by being able to use their new literacy and technology skills, gained through family literacy courses, to influence the content of the books their children read. What a remarkable sight it is to see Mienh and Hmong parents, who have never been literate in their own languages, telling stories to each other and recording the information in English on laptop computers to create books for their children!

In 1997, several Mienh parents, a language aide, and myself had the opportunity to present our literacy work at a statewide bilingual education conference. The story which the parents chose to present, the Mm Gou Tzum, ("the woman who can make things grow again"), is a legend about how Mienh people learned to grow rice. This story was recorded on a computer and transferred both to small books, which could be distributed to school children, and to a "big book," which a teacher could read aloud to a class. These books were beautifully illustrated in watercolors by school children and parents. Mienh parents rearranged the conference room into a circle of chairs, with a hearth in the center of the circle, represented by a rice cooker. They felt that it was important that the story be told rather than read, first in Mienh so that the audience could hear the sounds, then translated into English by the aide. They also felt that the audience must be served a bowl of rice while hearing it, since the importance of eating rice is central to understanding their story. It was remarkable to watch this group of Mienh people, who had not previously been participants in the literate world, negotiate the way in which they chose to tell their story to a professional audience.

Despite our attempts to record oral histories accurately, it became clear to us that cultural material is altered when it is enacted in a new context and through new technologies. The flip side of this process is that even when a project appears to accommodate immigrant ways, the immigrants involved still learn useful American skills. Our work in the Literacy Center made clear, that even when families re-enact traditional practices at a school site, such as slaughtering and cooking a pig for a celebration ceremony, the experience was altered by the setting. Conversely, the teachers were also altered by the experience. Watching 30 Mienh women prepare a feast of egg rolls, soup, and stir fry from a butchered pig in 4 hours of steady, efficient work opens one's eyes to levels and forms of cooperation foreign to highly verbal, individualized Westerners. The process required almost no verbal communication. People knew what to do and how to do it, and children and elders knew how to play their parts. Yet when we sat down to eat, female teachers ate with men, which would not have been done in a village setting; we sat at tables with chairs rather than on low stools; and the cooking was done on a gas range rather than an open fire. All of these factors created a new, rather than a strictly reproductive, experience. But even had we gone to lengths to reproduce exactly the setting of an Mienh village at festival, the reproduction would have been different than living it in the first place, since it would be enacted as a conscious choice rather than participated in as a matter of course.

A school–community garden was designed as an intermediate step— an intercultural space—between the world of school and the world at the Asian apartment complex. As in the family literacy project, the goal of the garden was to bring immigrant parents into the school through activities which built on their existing strengths and which supported their needs. Families were given plots in which to grow their own fresh produce, in exchange for sharing their horticultural knowledge with school children in a model Southeast Asian garden. The idea of building a Mienh garden house developed as a way for parents to show their children, and other community children, how they had lived in Asia. However, as we began to build, Asian building traditions came into conflict with school building regulations. Hence Mienh fathers, engaged as house building volunteers, were forced to make involuntary adjustments to American technologies. The following section describes how this situation developed.

CASE # 2: MIENH FATHERS ADAPT TO AMERICAN BUILDING TECHNIQUES IN THE EVOLUTION OF A MIENH-AMERICAN HOUSE

We must have the garden along with the house, and the house along with the garden. If one is missing, it will not look right or be right. (Personal communication with a Mienh elder, 1997)

Three Mienh men volunteered to take the lead in constructing a traditional field house in the school garden, to be used by school children for storytelling and other cultural activities. The eldest was a 61-year-old shaman and elder, who had built houses in Asia, but who could no longer do heavy work. The second was a 40-year-old father who had some house building experience before leaving Laos. The third was San Chow's son, who had had experience on American as well as Asian building teams. In addition to these men, the project required cultural brokers to create links between the project and the school. If one imagines a chain of players who can link best with those closest to them on the chain, one end would be would be an American architect hired to make sure the project conformed to school regulations, followed by me, the science project coordinator, followed by two Mienh and Hmong student teachers who could translate for the Mienh volunteers, followed by the Mienh volunteers themselves, and ending with the Mienh elders.

At the start of the project, the architect requested a model for the house. It was not traditional to construct such a model, so the student teachers attempted to construct one of Popsicle sticks. Unfortunately, it was not accurate enough to predict the problems which developed. The next challenge was gathering materials. Mienh houses were built of giant timber bamboo, which is hard to find in California, so we settled for saplings cut at a nearby ranch. The Mienh fathers justified this choice on the grounds that saplings are sometimes used in Asia, and that they are a readily found available, noncommercial material. When the saplings were laid out for the frame, however, the architect expressed concern at their irregularity, suggesting that some were not large enough to bear the weight of the house if children were to climb on it. The Mienh fathers were outraged, stating that we had sought their help as "experts," and were now undermining their expertise, and that no house in their village had ever fallen down. Furthermore, they stated that if children climb on houses, they deserve to fall down, and that this is what is wrong with child rearing in the United States. We expect bad behavior and we get it. They could never remember a child climbing on a house in their village, but if they did, they deserved to fall down.

Peace was finally achieved over bowls of noodles, and the men agreed to go and get more saplings if they were paid for their trouble. The fathers argued that "we have now become workers, not experts, and workers need to be paid." It was becoming clear to them that the project would be much more involved than they had expected. And they were right, because the architect's next demand was that the posts be cemented in the ground. Cement was a material that they had not used before and did not initially find necessary. Similar dilemmas occurred over using screws instead of vines to attach the house together, over roofing materials, and over many other things. Noodles had to be eaten on several occasions to preserve the peace. When it was time to put sides on the house, the elders insisted that giant bamboo be found. Mienh parents began driving around our city, using their hunting skills to find bamboo. Finally they located a back yard with a grove of bamboo growing along the river. We then had to negotiate with the owner, who luckily sold us 30 trees. The arrival of the bamboo made everyone happier. The Mienh fathers building the house had excellent skills with hand tools and created many beautiful features from bamboo, including intricately woven doors. School children came out each day to watch and help the progress of the house building, and teachers admired the craftsmanship.

At each step, Mienh elders and builders were pressed to adapt to American building practices or to give up the project. Neither the language aides nor I had realized the extent to which our idea of reproducing an Asian field house would need to change in the school situation. Many of the changes were not visible in the final product, because the fathers skillfully covered the cement with tamped earth, tied vines over the screws, and so on. However, the builders knew where the house deviated from their traditions. Initially this situation created a lot of tension. Mienh elders felt belittled by the challenges of the architect, and the student teachers felt embarrassed to be put in the position of criticizing their elders. A low point was reached when one of the key builders, having been told he must use cement, commented: "Now we are stopping building a Mienh house." However, as the house progressed, and the school children and teachers admired it, the builders became happier. One day the elder builder called me in to see a new cement floor he had poured on the bottom of a bamboo storage shelf in the house. "Cement, good," he said. I was amazed, since he had been most vocal in protesting cement foundation posts. I asked the Mienh student teacher to translate the elder's thought: "This house is not a Mienh house, but it is a Mienh-American house, just like our lives."

We were grateful for the generous spirit of this Mienh elder, who helped us to see what we had really been doing all along. Our purpose in building the house had been to create an historical reproduction, but what we really created was an intercultural structure, which like our lives, combined necessary parts from both worlds. The value of such a structure far surpassed our intentions. The house was transformative: it represented elements which had not existed before in either Mienh or American cultures. It was also symbolic of a peace, which the elders and the school personnel made with each other, to create something valuable for the children for whom they shared responsibility.

The Transformation of Products and Technologies in New Situations

Whereas the technological changes which the Mienh builders adopted while building the house were involuntary, we began to notice intercultural technologies used voluntarily by Mienh and other immigrant families in the garden and in our cooking projects. One day a Mienh mother came in to cook a traditional noodle salad with a classroom of third graders. The salad involved no less than 15 vegetables, herbs, and spices, most of them from the garden or an Asian store. As the final touch, the mother pulled a bottle of ranch dressing and a jar of peanut butter out of her basket. When questioned, she said that they had traditionally ground peanuts for this recipe, but that they had now discovered ready-made peanut butter. As for the ranch dressing, it simply tasted good. She had tasted it at a school pot-luck, and decided to incorporate it into her repertoire.

When immigrants use American products, they make them their own by creating new and innovative uses for familiar items. Ranch dressing in a spicy Asian salad is one example of these adaptations. Another is the way in which Asian parents use a variety of found objects to prop up plants in their gardens in the summer, and to cover delicate tropical herbs so that they can survive the winter. Parents find objects discarded in vacant lots and haul them into the garden. For example, fences between plots may incorporate an old spring mattress, junk wood, pruning from gardeners, and curtain rods. Similarly, the winter garden contains a makeshift greenhouse constructed from a child's plastic swimming pool, and a variety of other structures created from cardboard and plastic which serve the same purpose. Whereas some neighbors have commented that the use of found objects makes the gardens unsightly, we consider these objects a testimony to the creativity of Mienh parents as they attempt to make use of the cacophony of things discarded in a modern city. When the elder builder used the bag of cement as a floor in his hand-built shelves, he transformed cement from a compulsory material, which he was forced to accept, into a plastic material that he could use to forward his personal creative vision.

It is my belief that successful immigrants from rural areas like the Mienh are able to survive in an environment very different from their homeland because they are able to transform the objects they find in urban life in creative ways that serve their own cultural goals. Preliminary observations in Thailand suggest that the ability to piece unlikely things together to create a whole, a process called *bricolage* (Levi-Strauss, 1966), is present in people's lives in Thailand as well, and has merely been transferred to life in the United States. My own common sense interpretation is that subsistence people, accustomed to solving technological problems with materials they find, must be able to adapt materials to a variety of functions. Certainly in our community, the ingenuity of immigrants in using discarded material from mainstream culture to forward their own ends, far surpasses the skills of low income nonimmigrants in the same environment, and often is an important factor in immigrant economic success.

How Thailand's Development Affects Immigrants' Cultural Identity in the USA

After surviving our struggles about cement, screws, and the size of saplings, we approached the house-building meeting at which we would discuss materials for the roof with great trepidation. The "correct" roof for a Mienh field house is palm leaves, which are hard to find and require much labor dismantling palm trees. In addition, palm roofs have to be replaced annually, causing a labor demand the school is not able to meet. We were pleasantly surprised to find that the elders had already resolved the issue in favor of a corrugated tin roof. I could hardly believe this decision would come from a group that had opposed cement and screws. Why was tin technology suddenly acceptable? The answer turned out to be simple. Now in Southeast Asia, villages near the major cities use tin roofs. If a field house in Laos or Thailand can have a tin roof, then a field house at a school in Sacramento, California can have one too.

Mienh immigrants are acutely aware that villages and cities are changing in the homelands they left behind. This knowledge is a source of both happiness and concern, since immigrants from Asia, like immigrants from elsewhere, are often invested in the idea that the way of life back home continues as they left it. When Liew was preparing for our trip to Thailand, she told me that when she arrives at her village, she will put on her traditional costume and carrying basket, which she has not worn in many years, and will walk on the old pathways, not the new highway.

Many of today's immigrants maintain strong connections with families in their homelands. These connections affect their adaptations to life in the United States. For example, many Mienh families on welfare or struggling to live on minimum wage jobs, send money on a regular basis to family members still in Asian villages. Their sense of themselves as "wealthy" in relation to their relatives in the homeland provides them with an international perception of wealth and poverty, which is very different from that of their low income American neighbors, who compare themselves to richer people in the United States.

Creative Use of Technologies to Communicate Across the Ocean

Some of the most interesting adaptations in Asia that affect family members here involve communication technologies. Mienh and Hmong people do not have a literate tradition, hence it has been difficult for families separated by the Vietnam war to communicate by mail. However, village people have learned to make creative use of tape recorders. My daughter visited a Mienh village in Vietnam where people lived very traditionally, in houses with dirt floors, no running water, and no bathrooms. In the corner of their house, the shaman was instructing an acolyte in ceremonial chants, using a battery operated tape recorder. Similarly, Mienh friends send tapes back and forth between the United States and their villages. Because many villages have no postal service, it is common for whole villages to rent one post office box in the nearest city, purely for the purpose of receiving taped messages from relatives. When any village member goes to the city to market, he or she checks the post office box to see if anyone has received a tape. I think that this system represents an ingenious use of technology by a people who have bypassed the letter writing stage of development and moved directly from their oral culture to the second level orality of the tape recorder.

Another communication technology which affects immigrant youths is access to video and music tapes and cd's which are produced in Asia, then marketed in Asian stores in the United States. These videos and music tapes sometimes present traditional stories and music, but are most often examples of Asian movies and rock and roll, which mimic American trends in video and music. However, these products have their own twist, and are recorded in Asian languages. I was recently fascinated to witness three East Indian immigrant sixth grade girls performing at a talent school at an elementary school with an ethnically diverse student body. These girls performed two numbers in the show. In the first one, they appeared in saris and did a beautiful traditional folk dance. Ten minutes later, however, they had changed into jeans and tennis shoes and performed a syncopated break dance to a rock and roll recording from India. This recording was American rock and roll filtered through Indian eyes and ears, produced in India and imported to the United States, to be bought by Indian immigrants here. The same process goes on in Asian stores, where videos and tapes are available in many Asian languages. These imported products feed the Pan-Asian culture described above.

As the Suarez-Orozcos (2001) noted, immigration patterns early in the 20th century were marked by difficult communication with the homeland. Most movement was in one direction, with little chance to go back. In today's global economy, communication occurs in many forms: through media, including international cable TV, radio, tapes, cell phones, and increasingly, the Internet; through personal visitations via jet airplane; and through the exchange of products. Communication between immigrants and their homeland precludes them from imagining their culture of origin as static.

Communication also creates responsibilities that can be confusing or overwhelming for immigrants struggling to survive in the United States. The four children of a Mienh family with whom I work are paralleled by cousins, the children of their maternal aunts, who have remained in their village in Thailand and, in some cases, are asking to come here. How can the cousins in Thailand feel good about their own level of opportunity when every few months a tape recording arrives, telling of life in the United States? Yet is the answer for everyone to leave their homeland, or for all aspects of village cultures to modernize worldwide? It strikes me that there is much that modern society, on the brink of global warming caused by the overuse of certain technologies, has a lot to learn from villages, which have sustained themselves with little energy input for hundreds of years. Yet who will value this knowledge in the face of all the conveniences and opportunities which modernization brings?

ANALYSIS

Multiple Perspectives

The Mienh house exemplifies the notion of multiple perspectives, in that it represents many things to many people. Initially, it represented a cultural reproduction of life in Asia to the Mienh elders, parents, and Southeast Asian student teachers. Their dream was that their children could see what their lives had been like in Asia by looking at this house and the garden surrounding it. However, it should be noted that even when people were planning this historical reproduction, their relationship to it was not the same as it had been to house building in Asia. They were not building this house to live in, but rather to create a museum to their past lives.

As work on the house evolved, the tensions between traditional building techniques and school expectations created cultural conflict. Interestingly, the conflict resolved itself when a previously critical elder told us: "This is ... a Mienh–American house, just like our lives." This elder's statement helped us to redefine our project, which we had originally considered an historic reproduction, as an intercultural experiment.

The experiment did not end when the house was completed. The Mienh house took on unpredicted meanings for various people, some of which were different than those planned by its builders. A series of homeless men have moved into it, especially on rainy nights. For them it is a shelter. Simultaneously, diverse school children use it as a playhouse, investing it with meanings they bring from their own backgrounds. To city police, the house is an obstruction to surveillance of homeless people in the garden at night. Perhaps most poignantly, a Mienh parent told us that when she misses her country, she spends the night in the Mienh house. For her, it is a reminder of home.

Multiple Uses and Meaning of Technologies

Commentators often bemoan the effects of technology on modern children bombarded by media. In this study, the emphasis is reversed. Our interest has been in what we can learn from how immigrants coming from a nonmodern, nonWestern cultural perspective integrate, use, and make meaning of new technology tools. In other words, how does the perspective of the meaning maker affect the impact of the technology?

In this case, technology is defined broadly, to include any tools—from bamboo to books to computers—which people use to forward their ends. Each human technology emerges from a social context, but is potentially transformed as it enters new contexts. This transformation can take several forms. For example, bedsprings, discarded and placed on the street, can become a trellis in a family garden. Immigrants, liberated from preconceptions about bedsprings, are able to see them as woven wire structures, which can be used to support plant growth. In this case, the function of an object changes in relation to a new set of needs.

Acceptance of, resistance to, and mastery of technologies indicate immigrants' adjustments to their new culture. During the building of the Mienh house, fathers initially resented the intrusion of nontraditional technologies. Later, they accepted these technologies as appropriate to a Mien-American house, which, like their lives, represented an intercultural compromise. In the family literacy project, some Mienh parents learned to use laptop computers to record each others' stories. This new technology, coupled with their study of writing in English, enabled them to translate oral traditional knowledge into products, which could be used in the literate culture of school. It also enabled them to transform themselves from illiterate parents to authors, producing school curriculum materials. A similar kind of technology change occurs when tape recordings are used for communication with relatives in Asia. Tapes provide much more textured experience—including voice inflections, and even songs—than letters. They also enable illiterate elders to bypass the written word as a prerequisite for international communication.

What can we, as educators, learn from the way immigrants use new technologies? First, we can learn a lot from the fresh approaches to solving problems which immigrants provide. For example, teachers were surprised and pleased to see how immigrant parents made use of found objects as garden supports and how they saved and shared their own seeds. These skills enable them to spend less money on the school garden. It is also refreshing to open our eyes to new possibilities—to see urban trash as materials that can be recycled for other uses. In a world with limited resources, such lessons are important ones to teach our children.

At the interpersonal level, coming to understand how immigrant families solve problems enables mainstream educators to re-examine common stereotypes about the intelligence and skills of illiterate, nonEnglish speaking families. Teachers have little opportunity to alter negative stereotypes in the classroom, where immigrant parents lack the skills necessary to participate, and communication problems dominate the discourse. However, a new situation evolves when teachers garden, cook, sew, or build, with parents expert at these skills. Everyone is challenged, and everyone learns, from attempts to communicate across cultures and languages in the process of problem solving together.

Equalizing Power Through Community and Project Based Learning

Science and math educators place much emphasis on constructivism, defined as the way in which the learner creates meaning through experience. The school–community garden provides a living laboratory in which the processes discussed in discipline-based studies can be observed. For example, children can observe seasonal changes, plant and insect life cycles, erosion, and many other science concepts in action. In addition, they can grow pioneer gardens, study immigrant gardens, and process foods and fibers in the context of standards-based lessons in the United States and world history. When multicultural communities are present, the potential for constructivist learning is greatly enriched. Unfortunately, it is rare for schools to exploit this potential. Sometimes schools and other institutions are not prepared to change as quickly as society itself evolves. Four walls, paper and pencil tasks, education centered around the transmission of a static body of knowledge, and traditional teacher–student relationships lack relevance for urban children and parents who experience media and communication-rich environments in their daily lives. We need to develop educational settings which build on the knowledge which all parties bring to the situation, as well as the diverse international context in which we now live. Meaningful projects, such as growing food and building houses, coupled with the use of media and computer technology, provide contexts in which children and adults from different sociohistorical contexts can generate new ways of thinking and learning together.

There are several compelling reasons why schools should pursue community based, project based learning. First, it engages children and their families as producers of, as well as consumers of, knowledge. Second, it engages educators as learners as well as teachers. And finally, it places value on the funds of knowledge possessed by minority communities, including their technologies, by equalizing this knowledge with the "official knowledge" transmitted in schools. It makes education into an equal, intercultural exchange between groups, rather than the hegemonic transmission of the knowledge possessed by those in power. It is, in short, the education appropriate to a multicultural, democratic society.

Finally, constructivist models of education enable students, families, and teachers to take charge of the technologies available to them. Project-based learning creates circumstances in which immigrant populations in danger of becoming passive consumers of new technologies can become, instead, active producers of their own meaning making.

FINAL THOUGHTS

As we enter the 21st century, it is time to reconsider the accepted paradigms about human development in the past. Accelerated change—in mobility, in technology, and therefore, in cultural understanding—is a factor which has defined the 20th century and which promises to increase in the 21st. The phenomena described in this article are not limited to that small group of people known as the Mienh. Immigrants make up over one quarter of the children entering California schools each year, and "minorities," including Latinos, Asians, African Americans, and others, now constitute a majority of Californians. Furthermore, immigrants are not the only ones affected by rapid globalization and technological change. These changes affect us all.

In this article, I have argued that immigrants from developing countries interface with the technological societies, which they enter in complex ways, which cannot be explained by traditional notions of acculturation and assimilation. Whereas modern cities can be overwhelming to immigrants and natives alike, 21st century society is sufficiently dynamic to allow various individuals and groups to generate unique adaptations to it. Intercultural educational projects provide particularly rich opportunities for knowledge and power to be shared, for individuals and groups to resolve conflicts in creative ways, and for researchers to study how individuals adapt to change.

Finally, it should be noted that "high tech" interventions, such as the use of computers and video, and "low tech" celebrations of traditional skills and practices, can be integrated as complementary parts of 21st century life. Recently, while visiting a Mienh home, I listened to a tape, which my friend had received from her sister in Thailand. Her sister is illiterate, but composes traditional Mienh songs, which are improvisational poems sung in tones:

"When I think of you leaving Thailand by airplane, it was as if you went on a big silver bird, that rose into the sky. But when I look out of my window and see birds in the jungle, I know where they are going, and what their life is like. Yet I do not understand where your bird went, or what its life is like."

Through the medium of the tape recorder, two sisters have been enabled to communicate across the ocean, keeping alive a traditional form of communication that has become increasingly rare. It is our hope that technology can continue to be applied in ways that affirm rather than negate our diverse, multicultural world.

SUGGESTIONS FOR FURTHER RESEARCH

The literacy garden and house building projects described in the previous sections have caused me to rethink my own research in profound ways. The first step has been to move from programmatic research, centered on the testing of interventions and curricula, to narrative research, centered on the retelling and analysis of stories generated in intercultural educational situations. Narrative research is more appropriate to intercultural contexts because it is multi-dimensional, incorporating space, time, and interpersonal relationships. Is written text the most effective way to capture and communicate these multiple dimensions? Another issue affecting written research is the fact that it is not accessible to most members of minority communities. Even teachers rarely read formal research. My principal informant, with whom I went to Thailand, does not read English well enough to read the book we might author together.

These issues are leading me toward media-based research. For example, we might explore a web page format through which to present information gathered from the trip to Thailand. Such a format would enable people who do not read to access information through visuals, videos, and auditory effects. It could provide options in more than one language. It could enable children and families to access folk tales and photos, while providing more complex back-up materials for teachers. Ideally, it would enable children in Thailand to interact with their peers in California, and visa versa. This is becoming possible since even a small market town in most parts of the world has an Internet café. As we challenge schools to become more dynamic and relevant, we should apply the same standards to educational research. How such considerations will change research is a matter of further exploration, an exploration, which will inevitably require us to understand the relationship between multiculturalism, technology, and human development.

REFERENCES

Arellano, E., Tippins, D., & Nichols, S. (2000). Case-based pedagogy as a context for collaborative inquiry in the Philippines. *Journal of Research in Science Teaching, 38,* 502–528.

Boggs, S. T., with Watson-Gegeo, K., & McMillen, G. (1985). *Speaking, relating and listening: A study of Hawaiian children at home and at school.* Norwood, NJ: Ablex.

Clandinin, D. J., & Connelly, F. M. (2000). *Narrative Inquiry: Experience and story in qualitative research.* San Francisco: Jossey-Bass.

Goody, J. (1987). *The interface between the written and the oral.* Cambridge: Cambridge University Press.

Grove, P. B. (Ed.). (2002). *Webster's new international dictionary, Unabridged* (3rd ed.). Merriam-Webster, Inc.

Heath, S. B. (1983). *Ways with words: Language, life, and work in communities and classrooms.* Cambridge: Cambridge University Press.

Levi-Strauss, C. (1966). *The savage mind.* Chicago: Chicago University Press.

Lippard, L. (1990). *Mixed blessings.* New York: Pantheon.

Moll, L., & Gonzalez, N. (1992). Funds of knowledge in teaching: Using a qualitative approach to connect homes and classrooms. *Theory into Practice, 31*(1), 132–141.

Philips, S. U. (1983). *The invisible culture: Communication in classroom and community on the Warm Springs Indian Reservation.* New York: Longman.

Sleeter, C., & Grant, C. (1988). *Five approaches to multicultural education: Making choices for race, class, and gender.* New York: Falmer.

Suarez-Orozco, C. M. (2001). *Children of immigration.* Cambridge, MA: Harvard University Press.

Turner, V. (1974). *Dramas, fields, and metaphors: Symbolic action in human society.* Ithaca, NY: Cornell University Press.

MIND, CULTURE, AND ACTIVITY, *10*(1), 42–61

Toward A Framework for Culturally Responsive Design in Multimedia Computer Environments: Cultural Modeling as A Case

Carol D. Lee

School of Education and Social Policy
Northwestern University

This article offers a framework for the design of learning environments that takes culture explicitly into account. This article situates a rationale for the framework based on research in the learning sciences, cultural psychology, and cultural–historical-activity theory. The Cultural Modeling Framework is offered as an example of a culturally responsive approach to design. This article makes an explicit argument for the function of culturally responsive design in computer-based tools. It illustrates culturally responsive design in technology and its consequences for student learning.

The challenge presented in this article is for designers of learning environments to consider how cultural practices, especially among student populations of color and those living in poverty, may offer opportunities to improve the design of learning technologies. *Learning technologies* are here defined to include computer as well as non-computer-based tools, language use, and routine practices. This challenge is under-conceptualized in the field and under-represented in the array of learning tools available or under design. Most computer tools developed under the banner of constructivism honor the specific discipline into which students are being apprenticed, but assume a homogenous form of motivation that applies to any students, anywhere, anytime. Whereas there is a certain kind of efficiency to this approach, I argue there are also limitations. Equally important, there is little evidence that such tools are being used in schools serving students of color or students living in poverty. And where such tools may be used with students of color or students living in poverty, little attention is given to the impact of culture on how these tools are appropriated, especially in ethnically mixed groupings.

DESIGN AS A CULTURALLY RESPONSIVE PRACTICE

Design as a culturally responsive practice involves both the design of learning environments, broadly speaking, as well as computer-based tools to support learning. Design here takes as one of its goals apprenticing novices into expert-like ways of reasoning and problem solving. I position

---

Requests for reprints should be sent to Carol D. Lee, Northwestern University School of Education and Social Policy, 2120 Campus Drive, Evanston, IL 60208. E-mail: cdlee@northwestern.edu

culture at the center of such design because current perspectives view learning as changes in the quality of participation in cultural practices (Cole, 1996; Rogoff, 1990). These practices are historically inherited as traditions that are reinforced through institutions, such as the family, the church, the school, and the workplace (Brofenbrenner, 1979). These practices are also socially mediated and negotiated through interpersonal relationships among individuals in pairs and in groups (Lave & Wenger, 1991; Rogoff, 1994; Salomon, 1993). Traditions of cultural practices usually inhere in-group formations that have a historical character. Such group formations may be defined by ethnicity, language use, or occupation, among others. Although research in cognition and cultural-historical-activity theory have attended to cultural practices that eminate from disciplinary communities and work place settings (Engeström, Miettinen, Punamaki, 1999; Hutchins, 1995; Rogoff & Lave, 1984), very little attention has been paid to cultural practices based on membership in ethnic and language communities (exceptions include Cole, 1998; Cole & Scribner, 1981; Gutierrez, Baquedano-Lopez, & Tejeda, 1999; Lin, 1999; Nasir, 2000; Saxe, 1991; Serpell & Boykin, 1994). One goal of this article is to incorporate an attention to ethnicity and language use within our conceptions of principles of learning and by extension to principles of design.

RATIONALES FOR DIVERSITY IN DESIGN

There are at least four reasons for attending to cultural diversity in the design of learning tools. The label "culturally diverse" refers not only to nonWhite persons. All peoples have multiple communities and cultural worlds to which they belong, and it is important to consider their views and beliefs from their various points of view. The challenge for designers is to learn, much like anthropologists, what a target audience—majority or minority—knows and believes relevant to the learning objectives. However, in light of political inequities, this article emphasizes the importance of attending to the cultural worlds of students who have been traditionally underserved by public education and have been largely denied access to new computer-based technologies being developed to support complex problem solving. To illustrate each of the four rationales, I use examples grounded in funds of knowledge (Moll & Greenberg, 1990) embedded in cultural practices of African–American and Latino–American communities.

Rationale # 1: Building on Prior Knowledge

Both the cognitive and sociocultural literatures attest to the importance of prior knowledge. Activities are enriched when the learner can make connections between a new task and prior knowledge. Such connections help the learner to build more stable and situated understandings, increasing the likelihood that the learner will have resources to draw on in a conscious way when she meets an unfamiliar but related task.

Capitalizing on the prior knowledge of potential learners is no simple matter. In the Cultural Modeling Framework (Lee, 1997) that is discussed later in this article, we attempt explicitly to draw on the prior knowledge of speakers of African American English Vernacular (AAEV) in making links to specialized strategies and concepts in the domain of literary interpretation. The argument I make here is that there are valuable cultural funds of prior knowledge (Moll & Greenberg, 1990) that students of color and students living in poverty bring from home to the task of learning in school, but they frequently go untapped in the design of learning environments using computer-based tools.

Designers of computer-based environments can learn from the work of sociocultural researchers who have explicitly examined the cognitive consequences of participation in everyday practices and how that affects knowledge construction in school-based practices. This research includes, but is not limited to, my work in Cultural Modeling (Lee, 1993, 1995); the work of Pinkard (2000) discussed in a following section; Fuson's work in designing math curriculum at the primary level that nurtures funds of knowledge of Latino children (Fuson, Smith, & LoCicero, 1997); Moses and collegues' work in the Algebra Project which helps students make connections between everyday practices like riding an urban transit system and the nature of the rational number system necessary for transitions from arithmetic to algebra(Moses, Kamii, Swap, & Howard, 1989); the work of Saxe (1991) and of Nunes, Schliemann, and Carraher (1993) in examining the mathematical knowledge of poor children on the streets of Brazilian cities selling candy; the work of Rosebery, Warren and Conant (1992) in helping students make connections between community language practices and scientific reasoning; and the work of Moll and Greenberg (1990) in helping teachers make connections between the cultural funds of knowledge of Mexican American students and academic learning.

Often prior knowledge is viewed as generic and culturally neutral. I acknowledge the importance of naïve concepts or misconceptions. Such naïve concepts or misconceptions in physics, for example, may not be attributable to any ethnic group (at least within the borders of the United States), but are certainly useful in reform views on the teaching of physics concepts (Carey & Gelman, 1991; Minstrell, 1989). Thus this category of prior knowledge does not have to include a culturally specific focus. On the other hand, the studies cited in this section demonstrate that prior knowledge can be culturally sensitive. This view of prior knowledge is captured explicitly in the next rationale for culturally responsive design.

Rationale # 2: Cultural Models as Socially Constructed Ways of Knowing

Cultural models represent socially constructed ways of knowing. Our knowledge is organized as cultural models, with implicit ideas, attitudes, and values (D'Andrade, 1987; Rumelhart, 1980; Schank & Abelson, 1977). For example, our use of the phrase "going out to a restaurant" implies knowledge about how one carries out tasks, like getting seated, ordering, eating, and paying. People who share common cultural practices are likely to understand these cultural models and so there is no need, except for children and new comers to the culture, to explain them. Whole subdomains within academic disciplines try to understand these cultural dimensions of knowing. Fields like ethnomathematics (Ascher, 1991), ethnobotany, and ethnoastronomy have emerged in the last few decades in order to study systematically the relationships between the way peoples in different cultures conceptualize mathematics, botany, astronomy, and so forth; and what those conceptualizations say about their belief systems, that is, their cultural models of the world.

Black psychologists Jones (1980), Nobles (1980), and Boykin (1994) described cultural models that they argue persist in the African–American community and have African (particularly West African) roots. These researchers assert that African belief systems can inform the design of learning environments for African–American students. Boykin, for example, argues that African–American youngsters achieve well—that is, they are engaged and more likely to persist in learning—in environments designed to be responsive to what he calls an Afro-cultural ethos. I take the position in the Cultural Modeling Framework that as African American students engage in signifying talk (such as playing the dozens, i.e., "yo mama so skinny she could do the hoola hoop in a cheerio"), they invoke a set of strategies for comprehending and producing metaphors, irony, satire, and so forth. However, they also invoke certain habits of mind, including attitudes about language play as an aesthetically pleasing end, in itself. Thus, signifying for speakers of African–American English vernacular represents a cultural model about language use linked to literary constructs and strategies as well as a set of beliefs and attitudes. They come packed together. Understanding this package is important for thinking about design.

Rationale # 3: Supporting Engagement and Motivation

Perhaps the most widely used argument for attending to diversity in the design of learning environments is to support engagement and motivation in learning. Engagement and motivation are connected; they are displayed as a willingess to persist with effort. Mere opportunity to participate does not mean students will know how to participate. Nor does it mean that the roles and activities available will be sufficiently meaningful for students to want to persist. Much of this argument grows from Sociolinguistic research from the 1970s documenting the ways that discourse styles in classrooms limited forms and levels of participation by students whose community language differed from the so-called academic mainstream (Cazden, 1988; Cazden, John, & Hymes, 1972). With the new opportunities for forms of representation and communication afforded by new computer-based technologies, it may well be quite useful for designers to consider the implications of this work for communication opportunities within computer-based environments.

Rationale # 4: Supporting Social, Civic and Political Empowerment

Ladson-Billings (1994) said that education should teach students (a) to become culturally competent members of their communities of origin and (b) to learn civic consciousness; that is, to have a critical consciousness about how to work for power within our democracy. These goals are especially important for students living in poverty and students of color. Those who study gender in uses of technology (Bryson & de Castell, 1996; Kafai, 1996), identify equity as a goal of their interventions. Designers like Alan Shaw (1996) have explicit interests in empowering communities through use of computer technology. A recent report by the Benton Foundation (Goslee, 1998) shows the gap in educational uses of technology between low-income students and their more affluent peers. Again, the work of designers of noncomputer-based learning environments may well have important lessons for designers of computer-based learning.

CULTURAL MODELING DESIGN FRAMEWORK

Here I describe the Cultural Modeling Design Framework to illustrate how designers of educational activities might embody the rationales for culturally responsive design I have articulated. This framework has been used both to design curriculum that is not computer based and to design computer-based tools. I make this point to emphasize that the rationale for culturally responsive design is applicable with and without computer-based technologies. The rationale includes attending to prior knowledge and cultural models as ways of knowing to support engagement and motivation, as well as social and civic empowerment. In Table 1, I match each design step in Cultural Modeling with one or more of the rationales for culturally responsive design.

First, Cultural Modeling (Lee, 1993, 1995, 2000) requires a careful analysis of an academic domain and the relationships among kinds of problems within that domain. What content, strategies, and/or habits of mind are required? For a given sequence of tasks, what prior knowledge is required?

Second, those involved in design must consider what *prior knowledge* (including content, strategies, or habits of mind) do novices already have that may be related to what is involved in carrying out the task? What prior assumptions do they have about the activity structures and modes of interaction within the site of the practice? In the case of underachieving black and brown students as well as students living in poverty more generally, these last two questions are salient. When the curricular focus includes complex problem solving, the default hypothesis in public schooling is that such students bring few resources for learning disciplinary knowledge. This position is embodied in low expectations of teachers and institutional practices such as tracking. What forms of community funds of knowledge (Moll & Greenberg, 1990) that may be applicable to problem solving in the domain are rarely considered or even conceptualized?

In addition, student resistance to rigorous constructivist- teaching may be influenced by students' prior experiences in school (Hodges, 1998; Kindred, 1999; Matusov, 1996). Students who

TABLE 1
Cultural Modeling Design Principles

	Generic Design	Culturally Responsive Design Rationale		
	Task Analysis	Prior Knowledge & Cultural Models as Ways of Knowing	Engagement & Motivation	Social & Civic Empowerment
Cultural modeling design steps	• Analyze generative constructs in the domain. • Analyze problem solving based on expert-novice differences.	• Analyze cultural practices of target group and look for comparable models, analogies, naïve concepts, or misconceptions related to the academic problem to be solved. • Use existing cultural models, scripts, and schemas as models, analogs, or counter-examples to be interrogated by students.	• Structure learning activities in ways that invite students to be meta-cognitive, making their tacit thinking public. • Structure instructional talk using community based discourse norms, while incorporating discipline specific modes of reasoning.	• Identify content for tasks that invite interrogation of community and/or personal needs.

have worked in school for 5, 8, or 10 years have very well grounded beliefs about what people do in school. In contrast to current rigorous standards and focus on authentic project-based work, underachieving black and brown students and students living in poverty often have experienced school as a place where one is not required to think, to work hard, to raise questions, to take responsibility for one's own learning, or to challenge peers and teachers intellectually. Thus, the Cultural Modeling Framework requires that the nature of tasks, the sequence of tasks, and the nature of activity structures must take into account a wide variety of forms of prior knowledge and expectations that students bring.

Third, designers should consider the *motivational potential* of instructional discourse. In Cultural Modeling, we structure metacognitive instructional conversations. Because the assumption is that we are structuring activities that help students to make public to themselves and to others tacit strategies they already use outside of school, the focus is on talking about one's thinking. Although such conversations are difficult to manage, the idea is that undersanding how one reasons is inherently motivating. That is, based on motivational theories of self-efficacy, understanding what one is doing increases the likelihood that one will want to do it (Bandura, 1994; Weiner, 1985). In addition to metacognitive instructional conversations, the Cultural Modeling Framework also calls on designers explicitly to draw on community-based norms for discourse. Earlier work by Phillips (1983) and others (Cazden et al., 1972) demonstrates how norms for who can talk, how, when, and about what help to construct roles for participants to play. Lack of congruity with community-based norms for talk (including use of different national languages—such as Spanish; language varieties—such as African–American English Vernacular [AAVE]; or registers) has been shown to result in lack of participation in classroom talk. Rosebery, Warren, and Conant (1992) have repeatedly shown ways of apprenticing English as a second language (ESL) students into scientific reasoning by drawing on community based language practices and cultural models as anchors for instruction.

Finally, Cultural Modeling involves the strategic selection of the content of tasks. The task should be structured according to the cognitive demands of the domain. The content should also address community and/or personal issues, which if confronted, may open up doors for a sense of *empowerment*—personally, civically, and socially. The spirit of this objective is taken very seriously, for example, in the Algebra Project where mathematical literacy is viewed as a civil right (Moses & Cobb, 2001).

In the section that follows, I demonstrate the application of the Cultural Modeling Framework to the design of a high school literature curriculum that includes the use of a computer-based tool included as *one* of the artifacts in the curriculum design.

Reading Comprehension in Response to Literature: A Case of Cultural Modeling Prior Knowledge and Cultural Models as Ways of Knowing

In this application of the Cultural Modeling Framework, I elected to link a focus on prior knowledge with cultural models as described by D'Andrade (1987). In the rationale for culturally responsive design, I distinguished these two. In some reading research, for example, prior knowledge is viewed as generic knowledge structures. Such structures can include knowledge of strategies or tasks, none of which are associated with any particular ethnic group. On the other hand, in the rationale I also emphasize those knowledge structures that are associated with particular ethnic and language groups. Most curricular reforms today consciously consider students' prior knowledge, but rarely take into account cultural knowledge of particular groups.

Prior knowledge is a crucial element of reading comprehension. In the case of literary texts, particularly works of fiction, the prior knowledge may consist of any of the following categories of knowledge:

- Authors—their lives, styles of writing, other texts.
- Related texts.
- Traditions of criticism and the interpretive procedures attached to each.
- Allusions to real world events or images, symbols, etc. from other texts or media.
- Cultural assumptions about routine scripts of everyday life and social or psychological causes affecting the internal states of humans.
- Epistemologies about what response to literature entails.

Interpretations of literature may be enhanced or constrained by limitations in any of these forms of prior knowledge.

The Cultural Modeling Framework pays special attention to issues of prior knowledge and literacy teaching. One of the fundamental precepts of the framework is that culturally diverse students, often speaking devalued vernacular language varieties or first languages other than English, routinely use strategies for interpreting figurative language, irony, and satire as part of speech acts in their everyday communications. The current implementations of this framework have focused specifically on African–American adolescents and specific characteristics of the AAEV. There is a strong body of sociolinguistic research documenting the creative aspects of communication within the AAEV speech community (Mitchell-Kernan, 1981; Smitherman, 1977). I have claimed that, through participation in speech acts involving signifying, speakers in this community routinely interpret metaphor, simile, hyperbole, satire, irony, and shifts in point of view (Lee, 1993, 1997). Signifying is a form of talk that involves double entendre, indirectness, and is rich in figurative language, irony, and satire. However, as speakers of AAEV interpret these rhetorical tropes in common dialogues, they use tacit strategies. I have argued that the strategies are the same as those used in the interpretation of literature. As part of the routines in this framework, students are given what are called cultural data sets to analyze. These data sets may include stretches of signifying dialogue, lyrics from rap and R&B music, or videos (for example rap videos) with literary qualities. In each case, the cultural data set is one for which the students are presumed to have significant prior knowledge and which requires the analysis of some rhetorical trope or intepretive problem analogous to those that students will encounter in works of fiction in the curriculum.

METACOGNITIVE INSTRUCTIONAL CONVERSATIONS AS ENGAGEMENT AND MOTIVATION

A central activity structure within the Cultural Modeling Framework is the coordination of metacognitive conversations (Forman & Larreamendy-Joerns, 1998; Lee, 1999). These are discussions in which students are supported in making public the strategies they are employing as well as the evidence and reasoning they are using. In addition, such conversations involve interaction structures in which students initiate ideas, questions, and challenges, where instructional conversations are not solely directed by teacher's intentions. These modes of reasoning (i.e., publically articulating how you came to a position and evaluating your evidence) and modes of interaction (i.e., more than one person initiating ideas, questions and challenges) characterize avid readers of canonical literature. The norms for talk often involve overlapping multiparty talk, consistent with many AAEV discourse norms in speech events such as signifying, loud talking, and testifying (Smitherman, 1977). The initial modeling activities in units of instruction in the framework are intended to (a) draw out relevant prior knowledge of diverse underachieving students, and (b) socialize students into specific modes of reasoning and of interaction.

Many examples of modeling in the educational literature (Cazden, 1988; Palinscar & Brown, 1984) involve students observing a more capable expert reason and use strategies. In the modeling phase of the Cultural Modeling Framework, students actually participate in the form of problem-solving characteristic of the domain while they are still novices to the academic content. In this case, it means that students actively engage in interpreting symbols, irony, and satire (e.g., in rap lyrics) before they know what symbols, irony, or satire are, and before they are able to apply strategies for identifying or interpreting these literary tropes in canonical literature.

Task Content as a Bridge Toward Social and Civic Empowerment as well as Engagement and Motivation

African–American fiction provides the base of the curriculum because students are presumed to have relevant prior knowledge about their themes. The text sequence within any given instructional unit moves from modeling with cultural data sets, to texts of African–American fiction, and finally to texts from other traditions. All works share either interpretive problems or themes taken from the African–American core. The assumption here is that there are at least two categories of problems in response to literature. One involves knowing what kind of interpretive problem you are seeing in a text and having strategies available to generate a warrantable interpretation. The second involves making sense of the social codes in a text; that is, understanding, having some empathy (even if one eventually rejects the social codes) for what motivates characters to act as they do. Rabinowitz (1987) called this category assuming the role of the authorial audience, the audience the author assumed would know the social world the characters occupy. The initially selected African-American texts invite students to grapple with dilemmas related to racism, self-concept, and resiliency in the face of danger. Offering potential lessons for today, these texts provide spaces for students to explore the ways that African Americans have historically sustained themselves.

With this as a description of the kinds of experiences students had in the Cultural Modeling Response to Literature Curriculum, I turn to describe the Collaboratory Notebook (CBN), one of the tools that provided space and supports for their literacy learning. The culturally responsive curriculum and the CBN were part of an intervention in an underachieving African–American urban high school (Lee, 1993, 1995, 2001).

Cultural Modeling in the Design and Appropriation of a Computer-Based Tool to Support Literary Response

The CBN is a software tool originally designed by Daniel Edelson and Kevin O'Neill of Northwestern University for use in science education (Edelson & O'Neill, 1994). Professor Edelson and I cooperated on the redesign of the tool to meet the needs of the Cultural Modeling Project. The

CBN fulfills several functions. First, it provides hypertext links to sources of prior knowledge that can enrich the range of warrantable interpretations students may construct. Second, the CBN tool provides a structured environment for argumentative reasoning. Students are asked open-ended interpretive questions with explicit supports for articulating a claim, evidence for, as well as potential evidence against, a position taken. Third, the CBN tool supports collaborative thinking among students. In the first iteration of the tool, students were able to view responses to key questions made by other students and to respond to positions taken by others. The value of its use as a tool is that it is capable of including content that is relevant to different communities of students. Both the tool and the routines in Cultural Modeling classrooms presuppose that students will reason systematically, tackle complex problems, and collaborate. Both place the student at center stage, with the teacher's role as a keen observer of student thinking, one who shapes an environment, scaffolds students, and provides them with support flexibly as needed. Students do not begin to work in the CBN until after they have worked through the modeling activities using rap and other culturally familiar data sets and have begun to read the canonical texts.

USING CBN TO SUPPORT TACKLING INTERPRETIVE PROBLEMS IN *BELOVED*

The CBN is intended to make accessible to students a text-rich environment. Rabinowitz (1987) argued that expert readers use knowledge of the world and knowledge of other texts. The underachieving high school readers for whom these notebooks have been designed have not developed the disposition to read their worlds into canonical texts. For novice readers, this is especially true when referents in the literary work involve symbolism, irony, satire, or structural devices such as stream of consciousness or use of unreliable narrators. Our design of the CBN makes available to novice readers relevant associations for a section of a literary work. Students can then hypothesize meaningful relationships between the referent and its associations, using both the texts and their own personal knowledge as anchors for warranting their positions. Figure 1 includes the model for the rich text environment of the CBN.

Text passages are chosen because they pose a difficult problem of interpretation. They are ironic, satiric, dense with figurative language, or invoke an unreliable narrator. In any of these in-

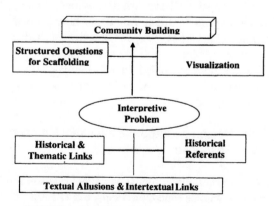

FIGURE 1   Building a rich text environment.

stances, a literal interpretation of the passage must be rejected and a warrantable explanation must add new layers of meaning beyond what is apparent. Although a range of interpretations is possible, any old reading will not do. A student must be able to justify her claim. She must link that claim to the wording of the text. The reasoning must reflect norms of literary criticism.

In the example, which follows, a stretch of text from Toni Morrison's (1987) *Beloved* is chosen. In this example, the protagonist, Sethe, describes her memories of having been raped and beaten during the African Holocaust of Enslavement. The scars on her back are described as a tree. Morrison also dramatizes the depth of Sethe's defilement from the rape and beatings. Sethe emphasizes how the rapist took her baby's milk, rather than her own defilement. She concentrates on the milk of the baby whom she would later kill to keep the innocent child from being taken back into enslavement. The CBN here focuses on images of the tree on Sethe's back, the scars on her back, and the relationship of Sethe as a nursing mother to her child, Beloved.

What follows then are linked pages, each with an image. Students are asked to hypothesize possible relationships between the selected text from *Beloved* and the linked images. They are also asked to provide information from the text that supports the associations they have made. They are asked to provide information from their knowledge of the world that explains why they made particular associations.

The ability to visualize while reading is an important skill (Sadoski & Paivio, 2001), especially in literature. The first linked page of an enslaved African in America with a scarred back provides students with a vivid visual image of Sethe's scars (see Figure 2). In addition, the metaphor of the scars looking like a tree takes on realistic and historic meaning when students see an actual human being living during the period of the African Holocaust of Enslavement who experienced the same savagery as Sethe. After each linked image page, an interpretive question is posed, asking students to hypothesize a warrantable link between the linked page and the text passage.

The second linked image is a West African Baobob tree. Its roots are so big they grow above ground (see Figure 3). The question attached to the picture of the African Baobob tree is what might this tree have to do with the tree on Sethe's back. There is no simple right or wrong answer, but, again, any old answer will not suffice. Whereas there is no evidence that Morrison had an African Baobob tree in mind when she constructed the metaphor of the tree in the novel, this particular image opens up interesting interpretive possibilities. This investigation may be viewed as an ill-structured complex problem. The strategies for solving this problem of connecting the Baobob tree to the text describing Sethe's back are applicable to other problems of symbolism.

The third linked page has a picture of a West African Nuba woman. The Nuba use ritual scarification for personal adornment and as initiation rites that signify to both the individual and the community that the initiate is a valued member of that community and ready to assume the responsibilties of adulthood, including parenting (see Figure 4). The Nuba woman in this picture is nursing her baby. On her bare breasts are scars, but unlike Sethe, these scars are signs of beauty. The scars signal her membership in the community. As a second ill-structured problem, the students are asked what might this Nuba woman have to do with Sethe and the tree on her back.

All the linked allusions just described involve pictures. The technology also makes it easy to use video images. In one part of the novel, Sethe remembers her early childhood when she had been separated from her mother. In her childhood memory, someone pointed out a woman wearing a hat and she was told this woman was her mother. At the same time Sethe is also remembering when she was about to deliver her youngest child, Denver, in the woods while escaping from the Sweet Home plantation. Sethe was in great physical pain. Her only help was a young White girl,

Amy Denver, who was also escaping from indentured servitude. Sethe describes the baby moving around in her womb like an antelope. In the next sentence, Sethe recalls herself as a child seeing her own mother and others on the plantation doing an African dance called the Antelope. In one of the links to this passage, the students view a short video of an African dance troupe. On the page with the clip is a description of the role that dance plays in traditional African cultures. Dance is a practice that reinforces a sense of belonging to a community. Ritual dance communicates and reinforces beliefs about human and spiritual relationships. Students are then asked what this video might have to do with Morrison's use of the antelope in the text. Such a problem provides students with additional supported practice in attacking ill-structured problems of symbolism in the text.

In each of the examples, we have been able to make use of unique capabilities of multimedia computer technology. Because the CBN is a tool, teachers, curriculum designers, or researchers can create content and interfaces that are responsive to the community of students and the particular demands of the texts. The Cultural Modeling Framework on which this curriculum is designed is culturally responsive in its conceptualization. This framework demands that tools, which sup-

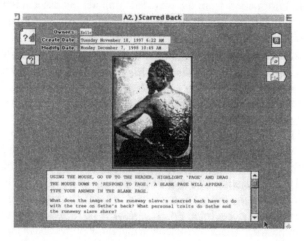

FIGURE 2   *Beloved* Collaboratory Notebook – Tree Symbol Link 1.

FIGURE 3   *Beloved* Collaboratory Notebook – Tree Symbol Link 2.

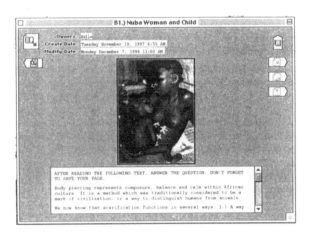

FIGURE 4   *Beloved* Collaboratory Notebook – Tree Symbol Link 3.

port it be culturally constituted. The tool itself is inherently flexible because it is simply a structure on which differing content and interfaces can be built. Secondly, the tool allows students to negotiate its use and their pace individually.

Interpretive questions were constructed in the CBN as a nexus of text passages, multimedia referential data, and one or more questions. The ways students used the CBN were enriched by the narrative nature of the multimedia data sets (i.e., pictures, songs, and videos that told stories) as well as the cognitive resources they were learning to draw on in the Cultural Modeling classrooms. Students often responded to these interpretive problems in culturally specific ways.

Sociolinguists (Smitherman, 1977) described the following features of AAEV discourse styles: use of direct address and conversational tone; verbal inventiveness, including unique nomenclature; rhythmic, dramatic and evocative language; use of sermonic tone and cultural referents. The literature on learning styles (Shade, 1982) describes African–American students as often field dependent, that is, interpreting a phenomenon from a more relational perspective. Table 2 includes examples of responses from students using the CBN *Beloved* notebook that reflect these AAEV discourse features. The particular statements reflecting each feature are underlined.

The placement of text passages, multimedia referential resources, and interpretive questions provided a problem space with special semiotic potential. The visual imagery in pictures and videos provided students with a hook on which to place what they imagined while reading. For example, one student writes, "In my head I could picture how Sethe's back would be and here I could see how it really looks. I see how it looks like branches." In the organization of their responses, one tends to see a procedural approach to writing about the links between the visual images, their imagination, their prior knowledge—either personal or historical—and the text. It is as if the organization of these problem spaces provides a kind of procedural and conceptual scaffold to help students work through the process of thinking through their responses. Although the image of the enslaved man's scarred back is a more direct link to the text, the image of the Baobob tree requires a more indirect, and therefore complex, inferencing to link to the text. The following response by one student provides a revealing example of how students thought out loud as they worked through the interpretive problems:

TABLE 2
African American Discourse Features

Direct address conversational tone

"Slaves ran away not only to be away of the cruelty they were suffering, but to be free. Slaves were considered chattel so nobody was human to the white man. For nearly 400 years, our ancestors paid the price for refusing to work, running away or trying to learn so they can be more than just a piece of property. When the fugitives slave laws was in effect the risk of getting caught for running away was very high. *Just in case you were wondering, at times they grabbed a free Negro and declaimed them as the escaped slave. Can you imagine yourself being whipped with cowhide.* A lot of slaves did not survive their whippings and others were completely traumatized for probably the rest of their lives."

"*In my head I could picture how Sethe's back would be and here I could see how it really looks.* I see how it looks like tree branches I would say they both got it by the whip maybe because they did something out of order or the slave owners probably had nothing else to do. So they did it for fun."

Verbal inventiveness, unique nomenclature

"Sethe and the slave share the same personal traits, because they were both whipped a lot in their life. *Sethe was messed with* just because she was pregnant, and the Slave was whipped just because he was a slave and for running away."

Rhythmic, dramatic evocative language; Sermonic tone; Cultural references

"I believe that Sethe was crazy personally because *ain't man on God's green earth going to scare me to the point I try to take my children's life.* Also I think after killing your child, seeing your son's eye come out of his head and his tongue chewed up, it ain't going to get you. Sethe seemed kind a sane on the outside but when you learn about her past you could understand why things don't bother her like they should. I think what drove her crazy is when schoolteacher had the boys take her milk."

Field dependency, involvement with the immersion of events and situations; personalizing phenomenon

"*I would compare Sethe to my mother.* The reason I use my [mother] is because she would do anything to help us from getting in trouble, or to let something bad happen to us. Just like Sethe killed Beloved, so that she would not become a slave."

The two-type of trees are very different to me, because the Baobob tree branches shows life all the years it has blossom[ed]. In the picture the tree shows kind of a hardship image. So in a way I have proved myself wrong, because now that I think about it the tree do remind me of Sethe's back. (CBN log H99; March 11, 1999).

The careful logic students used to construct warrantable links between the Baobob tree and the scars on Sethe's back, are exemplified in the following response by another student:

The similarities between Sethe and the tree's homeland is that they are both from West Africa. Sethe's roots also grow above the ground. Her ancestors were originally from Africa and they were taken from their native land and brought to America. Seeing that her ancestors were black that made fertile soil for her roots to spread, not that it was voluntarily, but her roots probably spread across the country, which is how she came to be in Kentucky.[1] Sethe is a leaf on her mother's branch.

If you compare all of this to the tree on Sethe's back, I guess you can say that the roots of the tree were a symbol of the pain and anguish that she endured in her life as a slave. You can also say that the

---

[1]The setting is actually Ohio, not Kentucky.

branches of the tree on Sethe's back were a symbol of the strength that she gained due to the pain and anguish she endured. (CBN log, H99; March 5, 1999)

First, it is clear that this student has continued to make links from the picture of the enslaved man's scarred back to the second Baobob tree referent. The CBN made it easy to move back and forth between data sets and to revisit one's answer to each question. Second, this student maintains across the answer an analogic stance that connects the two images and the text. She reasons metaphorically, as when she powerfully remarks, "Sethe is a leaf on her mother's branch." The student has clearly entered the cultural practice of literary response in her ability to hold simultaneously two competing, but complimentary interpretations; that is, the scars are both a symbol of pain or anguish as well as a symbol of strength.

The CBN allowed our team to make use of unique semiotic potential of digital technologies. First, the architecture of the tool allowed us the flexibility to create content that was culturally responsive to the students who would use it, while constraining a cognitive focus on argumentation. In addition, the process of creating that content itself sparked a learning process for teachers and university-based researchers together. This is consistent with the inherently dialogic nature of tool use (Cole, 1996; Vygotsky, 1987; Wertsch, 1991). We learned, students learned, the original designers of the tool learned, and the tool itself became appropriated in ways not originally considered by its designers. Something as simple as the sometimes satiric, sometimes metaphoric nature of passwords students created became interesting windows into the ways they personally appropriated the tool: *Mr. Big Boss, Infinite Dreams.* Second, the tool allowed students to manipulate media that would be difficult to access outside a digital environment. In those cases where students responded to video and audio data, they were able to control their access in ways not achievable if the teachers were showing the video using a VCR or music on a tape recorder. Of particular interest was how students exerted the flexibility of moving back and forth between cases, between multimedia data sets, in essence controlling their access in ways very different from what we saw in face-to-face discussions. This became particularly useful for students who had more difficulty in class or who would not compete for the sometimes competitive floor of classroom discussions. Students would literally talk aloud to themselves and to the computer screens, using a kind of egocentric speech in the Vygotskian sense (1987) to direct their internal problem solving processes.

OTHER CULTURALLY RESPONSIVE
DESIGNS IN TECHNOLOGY USE

The New London Group (1996) calls for 21st century multi-literacies because the medium through which much information is communicated is multimedia. Students must understand the hidden messages and points of view in visual, spatial, and audio media, with special sensitivities to language use and gesture. The group calls for conscious design work that attends to elements that are linguistic, audio, spatial, gestural, and visual. The group says that students must learn to take on multiple perspectives, to critique and understand competing points of view.

In many respects, Pinkard's (2000, 2001) position that we need to consider the cultural implications (i.e., engagement, taking on points of view, invitations for participation) of *interface design* is very relevant to the propositions of the New London Group. In the interface of "Say, Say, Oh Playmate," Pinkard (1999) addressed all five of the design elements raised by the New London

Group. What is communicated by this interface does seem to impact how, for example, little African–American girls see themselves within the subjunctive world constructed inside "Say, Say, Oh Playmate." See Figure 5 for an opening screet shot of "Say, Say, Oh Playmate."

In field tests of "Say, Say, Oh Playmate," Pinkard (1999) reported the response of two African–American girls working together with the program. Vernae and Shonda describe Sam, the imaginary little girl standing in front of the housing project on the screen in Figure 5:

> Vernae: Who's that girl? ...
> Shonda: That's Vernae ain't it? ...
> Vernae: She's pretty so it's going to be me (she points to herself and she has a big smile on her face).

Later in the same dialogue, the girls propose entering the imaginary house on the screen (based on the public housing project in which they lived):

> Nichole [Pinkard]: What you gonna do inside?
> Vernae: Eat (laughter). I did all of this work. Now it is time for you to feed me; then do my homework.
> Abby: You want to do your homework?
> Vernae: Yeah. What you think she [referring to Sam on the screen] has her bookbag for?

In addition to the interface, culturally responsive design should also consider the semiotic potential of the *activity structure*. Activity structures in our designs can be responsive to cultural diversity. Activity structures (Leontiev, 1981), including discourse patterns that are enacted within such structures, help to socialize participants into knowing what game is being played and what roles they are expected to play. What students' think they are doing has much to do with how they participate, how much effort they exert. For example, Gutierrez and colleagues (Gutierrez, Baquedano-Lopez, & Tejeda, 1999) acknowledged that one of the appeals in the Fifth Dimension Project (Cole, 1996) is that students see themselves playing games. Play is a powerful activity

FIGURE 5   Screen shot from Interface *Say, Say, Oh Playmate* (Pinkard, in press).

structure for children. Certainly the developmental literature and many best practices in early childhood education make this claim. Using the framework of goal-based scenarios (Schank, 1992), Pinkard's design in "Rappin Reader" and "Say, Say Oh Playmate" draw on activity structures that students from African–American low income urban centers engage in as routine practice, and which such students value as engaging. For "Rappin Reader," students are asked to reconstruct rap lyrics and to write their own raps based on patterns of songs in the system. For "Say, Say, Oh Playmate," students are asked to reconstruct clapping songs, such as Miss Mary Mack. Both programs teach early phonemic and word recognition skills. In field-testing both programs, students made statistically significant pre-post gains in sight vocabulary recognition.

In another sense, tools that are designed to help students program, such as versions of Logo and many of the programmable robots and tools being created at the MIT Media Lab (Papert, 1993; Resnick, 1994), also are based on the assumption that activity structures make a difference, especially in game format for children. Paula Hooper (1996) demonstrated the ways that students adapt such tools in culturally responsive ways. In Hooper's study, children brought their cultural models as resources to construct objects and represent people in an imaginary narrative world they created. Hooper conducted longitudinal research in an African centered elementary school in Boston where students used Logo Writer to develop programming skills and strategies in order to construct and animate stories they wrote. Hooper documented how students appropriated collaborative practices based on the principles of the Nguzo Saba[2] as resources in how they made programming decisions. In addition, Hooper has documented the AAEV discourse norms and cultural scripts the students incorporated into their narratives, including how they chose to animate characters and scenes. Hooper's research provides a fascinating example of the ways in which the openness and the power of the tool to support imagination can be culturally responsive. Students from very different backgrounds can all use Logo Writer to design representations of stories they want to tell in culturally specific ways, while they all are able to explore a common array of mathematical and programming ideas and procedures. This way of thinking about design relates well to Pinkard's (2000) argument for a common cognitive structure in the architecture of a computer-based environment, while allowing for diversity in terms of activity structures and interface. This is precisely what she has done with the Lyric Reader Architecture that underlies "Rappin Reader" and "Say Say Oh Playmate." The Lyric Reader Architecture allows designers to reinforce the same cognitive supports using different activitiy structures and different interfaces that are responsive to different audiences of users. This is different from a purely constructivist approach to design which implies that active engagement in open-ended activities are inherently engaging.

IMPLICATIONS

The argument of this article that the design of learning environments, including the use of computer-based tools, needs to take issues of culture into account is important for several reasons. First, a cultural orientation in educational design can contribute to our efforts to build situated theories of

---

[2]The Nguzo Saba are seven principles that form the foundation for the celebration of the African American holiday of Kwanzaa: Unity, Self- Determination, Collective Work and Responsibility, Cooperative Economics, Creativity, Purpose, and Faith.

learning. From the perspective of theory building, current orientations assert that participants, context, and task are important if we are to understand the complexity of learning and that our designs should take that complexity into account. The dominant cognitive research literature on educational design rarely specifically addresses the significance of whether players are African American, Puerto Rican, Mexican American, or Laotian, whether those players are speakers of English or persons for whom English is a second language or who speak a "nonstandard" variety of English. However, I argue that who these people are, how they culturally identify themselves, is not an irrelevant consideration in our design decisions. What we are to make of culture as experienced through ethnicity, race, and language variation—what knowledge, beliefs, goals emerge from these group based experiences—is not clearly understood. It is very important to acknowledge that the discipline of Black Psychology has addressed such issues for almost 30 years (Boykin, 1994; McAdoo & McAdoo, 1985; Nobles, 1980).[3] However, unfortunately, the dominant literature in the cognitive sciences acts as though this body of research simply does not exist. Very rarely do major "mainstream" texts with a cognitive orientation even cite researchers from the traditions of Black Psychology.

Second, this argument is important not only for the design of learning environments broadly speaking, but especially for the design of educational computer tools. There are a number of examples across disciplines of designers who have taken issues of culture into account, but do not involve uses of technology (Ball, 1992; Fuson, Smith, & Lo Cicero, 1997; Lee, 1993, 1995; Mahiri, 1998; Moses, Kamii, Swap, & Howard, 1989; Silver, Smith, & Nelson, 1995; Tharp & Gallimore, 1988; Zavlasky, 1996). However, there are few exemplars that involve the design or uses of computer-based educational tools (Hooper, 1996; Pinkard, 1999; Shaw, 1996). We know there are serious issues of equity in terms of computer uses in schools serving students of color and students living in poverty. Such students are more likely to have less access to high-end hardware and are more likely to use computers for low-level tasks. Yet, to assume that the many sophisticated constructivist, knowledge-rich, computer-based tools currently being used in schools are culturally neutral may steer us to miss important basic questions.

Third, the methods by which we evaluate how such computer-based tools are appropriated and their impact on learning, on the whole, do not take into consideration differential effects for groups that differ by ethnicity, race, language use, or class. It is quite possible that the tremendous funding being invested in the development of such computer-based tools in education may be simply reinforcing current inequities in opportunities to learn, unintentionally widening the achievement gap.

Finally, I want to respond to an often cited critique of culturally responsive approaches—that is, that it is cumbersome, if not impossible, to address the breadth of cultural diversity, for example, within the United States. In this case, computer-based technologies offer unique opportunities. Computer-based tools can provide underlying architectures that allow for multiple forms of modeling, of ways that learners can represent their understanding, and multiple routes for interactivity and appropriation. In the case of tools such as the Lyric Architecture developed by Pinkard (2000) and the CBN described in this article, teachers, for example, can create content, structure tasks, and in some cases create interfaces that can be adapted to local audiences. In the case of such tools as Logo Writer, as demonstrated by Hooper (1996), students can appropriate the

---

[3]The *Journal of Black Psychology* has been a major source for publishing research in Black Psychology.

tools for representation—sounds, images, opportunities to create colors and shapes, and so forth—and methods of interaction that are responsive to cultural differences.

The proposition for design as a culturally responsive practice and the example of the Cultural Modeling Framework are intended to at least suggest that our fundamental understandings about learning and about uses of technology to support learning can be expanded meaningfully by at least placing the question of culture at the center of our practice.

ACKNOWLEDGMENTS

The research for this article was supported by grants to the author from the Spencer Foundation and the McDonnell Foundations Cognitive Studies in Educational Practice. An earlier version of this article was presented as part of an AERA panel. The chair and disscussant of that panel was to have been Jan Hawkins before her untimely transition. Xiaodong Lin and I had discussed the idea of the panel with Jan because of Jan's long commitment to issues of equity and cultural diversity in terms of technology in education. This special issue is a well-deserved tribute to her legacy.

REFERENCES

Ascher, M. (1991). *Ethnomathematics: A multicultural view of mathematical ideas.* Pacific Grove, CA: Brooks/Cole.

Ball, A. F. (1992). Cultural preferences and the expository writing of African-American adolescents. *Written Communication, 9*(4), 501–532

Boykin, A. W. (1994). Harvesting culture and talent: African American children and educational reform. In R. Rossi (Ed.), *Educational reform and at risk students* (pp. 116–138). New York: Teachers College Press.

Brofenbrenner, U. (1979). *The ecology of human development: Experiment by nature and design.* Cambridge, MA: Harvard University Press.

Bryson, M., & de Castell, S. (1996). Learning to make a difference: Gender, new technologies, and in/equity. *Mind, Culture, and Activity, 3,* 119–135.

Carey, S., & Gelman, R. (1991). *The epigenesis of mind: Essays on biology and cognition.* Hillsdale, NJ: Lawrence Erlbaum Associates, Inc.

Cazden, C. (1988). *Classroom discourse: The language of teaching and learning.* Portsmouth, NH: Heinemann.

Cazden, C., John, V. P., & Hymes, D. (1972). *Functions of language in the classroom.* New York: Teachers College Press.

Cole, M. (1996). *Cultural psychology: A once and future discipline.* Cambridge, MA: Belknap/Harvard University Press.

Cole, M. (1998). Can cultural psychology help us think about diversity? *Mind, Culture, and Activity, 5,* 291–304.

Cole, M., & Scribner, S. (1981). *The psychology of literacy.* Cambridge, MA: Harvard University Press.

D'Andrade, R. (1987). A folk model of the mind. In D. Holland & N. Quinn (Eds.), *Cultural models in language and thought* (pp. 112–147). New York: Cambridge University Press.

Edelson, D. C., & O'Neill, D. K. (1994). The co-vis collaboratory notebook: Supportive collaborative scientific inquiry. *Proceedings of the National Educational Computing Conference* (pp. 146–152). Eugene, OR: International Society for Technology in Education.

Engeström, Y., Miettinen, R., & Punamaki, R.-L. (1999). *Perspectives on activity theory.* New York: Cambridge University Press.

Forman, E., & Larreamendy-Joerns, J. (1998). Making explicit the implicit: Classroom explanations and conversational implicatures. *Mind, Culture, and Activity, 5,* 105–113.

Fuson, K., Smith, S., & LoCicero, A. (1997). Supporting Latino first graders' ten-structured thinking in urban classrooms. *Journal for Research in Mathematics Education, 28,* 738–760.

Goslee, S. (1998). *Losing ground bit by bit: Low-income communities in the information age.* Washington, DC: Benton Foundation.

Gutierrez, K., Baquedano-Lopez, P., & Tejeda, C. (1999). Rethinking diversity: Hybridity and hybrid language practices in the Third Space. *Mind, Culture, and Activity, 6,* 286–303.

Hodges, D. C. (1998). Participation as dis-identification with/in a community of practice. *Mind, Culture, and Activity, 5,* 272–290.

Hooper, P. K. (1996). "They have their own thoughts": A story of constructivist learning in an alternative African-centered community school. In Y. Kafai & M. Resnick (Eds.), *Constructionism in practice: Designing, thinking, and learning in a digital world* (pp. 241–255). Mahwah, NJ: Lawrence Erlbaum Associates, Inc.

Hutchins, E. (1995). *Cognition in the wild.* Cambridge, MA: MIT Press.

Jones, R. (1980). *Black psychology.* New York: Harper & Row.

Kafai, Y. B. (1996). Electronic play worlds: Gender differences in children's construction of video games. In Y. B. Kafai (Ed.), *Constructionism in practice: Designing, thinking, and learning in a digital world* (pp. 97–124). Mahwah, NJ: Lawrence Erlbaum Associates, Inc.

Kindred, J. B. (1999). "8/18/97 Bite me": Resistance in learning and work. *Mind, Culture, and Activity, 6,* 196–221.

Ladson-Billings, G. (1994). *The dreamkeepers.* San Francisco: Jossey-Bass.

Lave, J., & Wenger, E. (1991). *Situated learning.* New York: Cambridge University Press.

Lee, C. D. (1993). *Signifying as a scaffold for literary interpretation: The pedagogical implications of an African American discourse genre* (Research Report Series). Urbana, IL: National Council of Teachers of English.

Lee, C. D. (1995). A culturally based cognitive apprenticeship: Teaching African American high school students' skills in literary interpretation. *Reading Research Quarterly, 30*(4), 608–631.

Lee, C. D. (1997). Bridging home and school literacies: A model of culturally responsive teaching. In J. Flood, S. B. Heath, & D. Lapp (Eds.), *A handbook for literacy educators: Research on teaching the communicative and visual arts* (pp. 330–341). New York: Macmillan.

Lee, C. D. (1999). *Supporting the development of interpretive communities through metacognitive instructional conversations in culturally diverse classrooms.* Paper presented at the Annual Meeting of the American Educational Research Association, Montreal, Canada.

Lee, C. D. (2000). Signifying in the zone of proximal development. In C.D. Lee, & P. Smagorinsky (Eds.), *Vygotskian perspectives on literacy research: Constructing meaning through collabative inquiry* (pp. 191–225). New York: Cambridge University Press.

Lee, C. D. (2001). Is October Brown Chinese? A cultural modeling activity system for underachieving students. *American Educational Research Journal, 38*(1), 97–142.

Leontiev, A. N. (1981). The problem of activity in psychology. In J. V. Wertsch (Ed.), *The concept of activity in Soviet psychology* (pp. 37–71). Armonk, NY: Sharpe.

Lin, X. (1999). *Cultural continuity and technology artifacts: A case study of a 5th grade Hong Kong classroom.* Paper presented at the Annual Meeting of the American Educational Research Association, Montreal, Canada.

Mahiri, J. (1998). *Shooting for excellence: African American and youth culture in new century schools.* New York: Teachers College Press and National Council of Teachers of English.

Matusov, E. (1996). Intersubjectivity without agreement. *Mind, Culture, and Activity, 3,* 25–45.

McAdoo, H. P., & McAdoo, J. L. (Eds.). (1985). *Black children: Social, educational and parental environments.* Beverly Hills, CA: Sage.

Minstrell, J. (1989). Teaching science for understanding. In L. B. Resnick & L. E. Klopfer (Eds.), *Toward the thinking curriculum current cognitive research* (pp. 129–149). Alexandria, VA: ASCD Books.

Mitchell-Kernan, C. (1981). Signifying, loud-talking and marking. In A. Dundes (Ed.), *Mother wit from the laughing barrel* (pp. 310–328). Englewood, Cliffs, NJ: Prentice Hall.

Moll, L., & Greenberg, J. B. (1990). Creating zones of possibilities: Combining social contexts for instruction. In L. Moll (Ed.), *Vygotsky and education: Instructional implications and applications of sociohistorical psychology* (pp. 319–348). New York: Cambridge University Press.

Morrison, T. (1987). *Beloved.* New York: Alfred A. Knopf.

Moses, R. P., & Cobb, C. (2001). *Radical equations: Math literacy and civil rights.* Boston, MA: Beacon.

Moses, R. P., Kamii, M., Swap, S. M., & Howard, J. (1989). The algebra project: Organizing in the spirit of Ella. *Harvard Educational Review, 59*(4), 423–443.

Nasir, N. (2000). "Points ain't everything": Emergent goals and average and percent understandings in the play of basketball among African-American students. *Anthropology and Education Quarterly, 31,* 283–305.

Nobles, W. (1980). African philosophy: Foundations for Black psychology. In R. L. Jones (Ed.), *Black psychology* (2nd ed., pp. 23–36). New York: Harper & Row.

Nunes, T., Schliemann, A. D., & Carraher, D. W. (1993). *Street mathematics and school mathematics.* New York: Cambridge University Press.

Palinscar, A., & Brown, A. (1984). Reciprocal teaching of comprehension- fostering and comprehension-monitoring strategies. *Cognition and Instruction, 2*(2), 73–109.

Papert, S. (1993). *The children's machine*. New York: Basic Books.

Phillips, S. U. (1983). *The invisible culture: Communication in classroom and community on the Warm Springs Indian Reservation*. New York: Longman.

Pinkard, N. (1999). *Learning to read in culturally responsive computer environments*. Ann Arbor, MI: Center for the Improvement of Early Reading Achievement.

Pinkard, N. (2000). Lyric reader: Architecture for creating intrinsically motivating and culturally relevant reading environments. *Interactive Learning Environments, 7*, 1–30.

Pinkard, N. (2001). Rappin' Reader and Say Say Oh Playmate: Using children's childhood songs as literacy scaffolds in computer based learning environments. *Journal of Research on Computers in Education, 25*(1).

Rabinowitz, P. (1987). *Before reading: Narrative conventions and the politics of interpretation*. Ithaca, NY: Cornell University Press.

Resnick, M. (1994). *Turtles, termites and traffic jams: Exporations in massively parallel microworlds*. Cambridge, MA: MIT Press.

Rogoff, B. (1990). *Apprenticeship in thinking: Cognitive development in social context*. New York: Oxford University Press.

Rogoff, B. (1994, Fall). Developing understanding in the idea of communities of learners. *Mind, Culture, and Activity, 1*, 209–229.

Rogoff, B., & Lave, J. (Eds.). (1984). *Everyday cognition: Its development in social context*. Cambridge, MA: Harvard University Press.

Rosebery, A. S., Warren, B., & Conant, F. R. (1992). Appropriating scientific discourse: Findings from language minority classrooms. *The Journal of Learning Sciences, 2*(1), 61–94.

Rumelhart, D. (1980). Schemata: The building blocks of cognition. In R. Spiro, B. Bruce, & W. Brewer (Eds.), *Theoretical issues in reading comprhension*, (pp. 33–58). Hillsdale, NJ: Lawrence Erlbaum Associates, Inc.

Sadoski, M., & Paivio, A. (2001). *Imagery and text: A dual coding theory of reading writing*. Mahwah, NJ: Lawrence Erlbaum Associates, Inc.

Salomon, G. (1993). *Distributed cognitions: Psychological and educational considerations*. New York: Cambridge University Press.

Saxe, G. (1991). *Culture and cognitive development: Studies in mathematical understanding*. Hillsdale, NJ: Lawrence Erlbaum Associates, Inc.

Schank, R. (1992). *Goal-based scenarios (Technical Report No. 36)*. Evanston, IL: Institute for the Learning Sciences/Northwestern University.

Schank, R., & Abelson, R. (1977). Scripts, plans, goals, and understanding. Hillsdale, NJ: Lawrence Erlbaum Associates, Inc.

Serpell, R., & Boykin A. (1994). Cultural dimensions of cognition: A multiplex, dynamic system of constraints and possibilities. In R. J. Sternberg (Ed.), *Thinking and problem solving* (pp. 369–408). San Diego, CA: Academic.

Shade, B. (1982). Afro-American cognitive style: A variable in school success. *Review of Educational Research, 52*, 219–244.

Shaw, A. (1996). Social constructionism and the inner city: Designing environments for social development and urban renewal. In Y. Kafai (Ed.), *Constructionism in practice: Designing, thinking, and learning in a digital world* (pp. 175–206). Mahwah, NJ: Lawrence Erlbaum Associates, Inc.

Silver, E., Smith, M. S., & Nelson, B. S. (1995). The QUASAR Project: Equity concerns meet mathematics education reform in the middle school. In W. Secada, E. Fennema, & L. B. Adajian (Eds.), *New directions for equity in mathematics education* (pp. 9–56). New York: Cambridge University Press.

Smitherman, G. (1977). *Talkin and testifyin: The language of Black America*. Boston: Houghton Mifflin.

Tharp, R., & Gallimore, R. (1988). *Rousing minds to life: Teaching, learning, and schooling in social context*. New York: Cambridge University Press.

The New London Group. (1996). A Pedagogy of multiliteracies: Designing social futures. *Harvard Educational Review, 66*, 60–92.

Vygotsky, L. (1987). *Thinking and speech*. New York: Plenum.

Weiner, B. (1985). An attributional theory of achievment motivation and emotion. *Psychological Review, 92*, 548–573.

Wertsch, J. (1991). *Voices of the mind: A sociocultural approach to mediated action*. Cambridge, MA: Harvard University Press.

Zaslavsky, C. (1996). *The multicultural math classroom*. Portsmouth, NH: Heinemann.

MIND. CULTURE. AND ACTIVITY. *10*(1). 62–79

The Impact of Internet Use on Relationships Between Teachers and Students

Janet Ward Schofield
University of Pittsburgh

Ann Locke Davidson
Educational Connections

A 5-year primarily qualitative study of a major effort to bring the Internet to a large urban school district in the United States suggests that Internet use brought about unplanned as well as planned change in classroom roles and relationships. Specifically, it increased student autonomy, due to factors including increased student access to external resources, technical difficulties arising when students all tried to do the exact same thing on the Internet, and a reversal of the usual knowledge disparity between teachers and students. Internet use also frequently resulted unexpectedly in warmer and less adversarial teacher–student relations, due to factors including the tendency for Internet use to lead to small group work which in turn personalized student–teacher relations, increased student enjoyment and motivation, teachers' discovery of unexpected Internet skills on the part of students who had not otherwise impressed them, and increased autonomy, which influenced the affective tone of student–teacher relations in direct and indirect ways.

Computers are not just tools that perform expected functions in classrooms in completely predictable ways (Hativa, 1994). Their use in schools, as in other organizations, is both affected by existing social arrangements and relationships and impacts such arrangements and relations in planned and unplanned ways (Kling, 1996; Mantovani & Spagnolli, 2000; Schofield, 1995; 1997). Understanding the complex reciprocal relationship between computer use and the social functioning of classrooms is crucial to understanding the impact of the use of computer technology on education. For example, early work in this area by Jan Hawkins and her colleagues points to the importance of understanding the relationship between how teachers conceptualize the purpose of computer software and their use of it (Hawkins, 1987; Sheingold, Hawkins & Char, 1984). Other related work suggests that computer use can strongly influence the degree to which students collaborate with their peers, which in turn may well influence what and how they learn (Hawkins, 1984).

Following in the tradition of such work, this article highlights the importance of paying close attention to the ways that using the Internet creates planned and especially unplanned changes in the social functioning of classrooms. In addition, it suggests the importance of understanding how Internet use plays out in practice and the degree to which it enhances or detracts from the classroom environment. Specifically, this article explores the ways in which Internet use increased the

Requests for reprints should be sent to Janet Ward Schofield, 517 LRDC, 3939 O'Hara Street, University of Pittsburgh, Pittsburgh. PA 15260. E-mail: schof@pitt.edu

degree of independence that students experienced and improved the affective tone of student–teacher relationships in the classrooms of a large urban school district.

We focus on these two changes for several reasons. First, these two aspects of classroom life were very commonly influenced by Internet use in the schools we studied. Second, our research suggests that these two aspects of classroom roles and relationships are interrelated, which underlines the importance of exploring both the direct and the indirect effects of changes stemming from Internet use. Third, since the first change was planned by a small subset of teachers but appeared in many classrooms and the other was completely unplanned, consideration of these particular changes highlights the importance of recognizing the unplanned impact of Internet use. Fourth, both changes have potentially important implications.

Prior to describing these changes and their origins, it should be noted that this study was carried out in an urban context in the United States. The changes we describe here were not particular to one ethnic group or gender in this context. However, Internet use could play out quite differently in another national setting or even within a different context within the United States. Taking one example, we found that students generally valued and embraced the increased autonomy they experienced while working online. Teachers too, even those who initially attempted to implement practices designed to lessen the degree to which students' autonomy was increased, tended to feel quite positively about this change. This is not particularly surprising in light of the fact that independence and initiative are fostered in European American children in the U.S. from an early age and that self-control tends to be promoted and valued in American school children (see, e.g., Greenfield, 1994; Heath, 1993; Lebra, 1994; Spindler & Spindler, 1987). As we discuss, although American schools have been criticized for their tendency toward whole-group, recitation-based teaching and teacher-direction (Goodlad, 1984, Tharp & Gallimore, 1991), they do tend to value individual achievement and development relative to schools found in some other cultures (Greenfield, 1994; Spindler & Spindler, 1987). It is certainly possible, therefore, that the changes we discuss here would be received differently elsewhere. Also, teachers in other cultures might implement Internet use in a very different manner than did teachers in the schools studied.

Having said this, research conducted within the United States suggests that the changes we describe are likely to be seen as desirable by many. For example, increased perception of autonomy and control by students in the United States appears to increase their motivation (Ames, 1990; Schofield, 1995). Further, feelings of being in control are related to students' positive attitudes toward school (Henderson & Dweck, 1990). Finally, current theory in education suggests that learning may be enhanced through practices such as allowing students to try out their own procedures for solving problems, to pursue their personal interests, to contribute to the assessment of their own work, and to help plan classroom activities. All of these practices give students a more independent and powerful role in classrooms than they typically have now (Ravitz, Becker, & Wong, 2000). Although students in this study nearly always enjoyed increased independence, they did not always use it wisely. Thus, this research suggests that the likely impact of increased autonomy on students' learning may well be mixed.

The affective tone of the teacher–student relationship is also an important aspect of classrooms, for teachers as well as for students, and improving such relationships may well have important positive consequences. For example, Lortie's (1975) classic study of American teachers concludes that "the mastery of interpersonal processes ... can be seen as close to the heart of respondents' definitions of high performance in their craft" (p. 118–119). It also reports that teachers see good teacher–student relations as useful in facilitating classroom management, and ultimately in creating a climate conducive to learning. Goodlad (1984) reinforces the importance of the affective tone of teacher–student relationships by concluding that student and teacher satisfaction tends to be high in schools with positive classroom climates, of which positive teacher–student relationships constitute one dimension. The nature of interpersonal relationships between teachers and students influences students' motivation towards and interest in school as well as to in particular classes, with more positive relationships leading to increased interest in school as well as positive academic motivation and achievement (Wentzel, 1998; Wentzel & Wigfield, 1998). Teacher–student relationships have also been related to a feeling of school belonging, which in turn helps to predict students' academic achievement (Roeser, Midgley, & Urdan, 1996). In addition, at-risk students from a variety of backgrounds tend to speak ardently about the importance of connecting meaningfully with teachers who demonstrate interest in students as individuals (Davidson, 1999; Wehlage & Rutter, 1986).

THE STUDY CONTEXT:
NETWORKING FOR EDUCATION TESTBED[1] (NET)

The data on which this article were collected during a larger study of Internet implementation in a major urban school district is based in a working-class community. Roughly 55% of the district's students are African American. Most of the remaining 45% are European American. Although many of the district's students are from backgrounds of quite low socioeconomic status, which is often associated with relatively poor performance on standardized tests, its students, especially the younger ones, perform roughly at the national average on such tests. Thus, the district is generally considered have a viable school system and it enjoys a reasonable measure of public support.

In the mid 1990s, the National Science Foundation funded the Networking for Education Testbed. NET was a collaboration among the district, a federally funded supercomputing center, and a local university to bring Internet access to district students. NET's primary goal was to foster teacher-initiated, curriculum-based Internet use. To achieve this goal, after the pilot project year, teachers were invited to form school-based teams and to apply for Internet access via a proposal process. A committee consisting of representatives of the major stakeholders in the district selected the proposals it felt were most promising. By the end of NET's 5-year life span, teams of educators from 29 schools were participating. The Internet activities stimulated by NET varied tremendously. Some focused on a particular discipline, whereas others were interdisciplinary; some conceptualized the Internet as an information archive, whereas others used it primarily for communicative purposes; some were long-term projects, whereas others were short-term; many were conducted in regular classrooms, but some were conducted in computer labs. In spite of these differences, projects were similar in that they were teacher-generated and implemented in a context that provided a substantial amount of both Internet related professional development and ongoing technical support.

The data on which this article is based are drawn from a study conducted within the 10 schools that joined NET during its first and second years in order to conduct Internet-based curricular projects. The very large majority of these data come from a subset of five schools, two elementary

---

[1]Pseudonyms are used for the Internet project studied and for all individuals, institutions, and places to protect the confidentiality of those participating in this research.

schools, one middle school, and two high schools, in which we conducted intensive case studies. Data from the remaining five schools were used to refine, corroborate, and extend the case study findings. We studied schools joining NET in its first 2 years because it was in these schools that we had the opportunity to study change over a several year period rather than just in its earliest phase when schools were being wired and teachers often struggled with technical problems and with discovering how and if their initial plans for Internet use worked.

METHODS

The major data-gathering methods used were qualitative observation, semi-structured interviews, the collection of archival material, and the administration of questionnaires and surveys. Observational data were gathered during more than 230 class sessions in over 35 classrooms in which the Internet was being used. Trained observers used the "full field note" method of data collection (Olson, 1976), which involves taking extensive hand-written notes. Semi-structured open-ended interviews were conducted with 128 educators and 76 students from the five case study schools.[2] Students interviewed were diverse in terms of both gender and race. Both field notes and interviews were audio taped, transcribed, and coded. In the analysis of these materials, the primary emphasis was on developing and systematically applying thematic categories. In addition, interviews were also analyzed in a more quantitative-manner, using an approach that Kvale (1996) calls *meaning categorization.*

Archival materials were another useful source of information. For example, using a meaning categorization analysis similar to the approach used when analyzing interviews, we analyzed the proposals submitted by educators wishing to join NET. We also administered close-ended questionnaires to 95 students from elementary, middle, and high schools. These quantitative data, as well as teacher survey and questionnaire data, were analyzed using descriptive and inferential statistics.

In drawing conclusions, close attention was paid to triangulating data from individuals occupying different roles in the school system as well as data gathered by different methods. For more methodological details see Schofield and Davidson (2002).

INCREASED STUDENT AUTONOMY IN THE CLASSROOM

A variety of data indicate that students often experienced increased independence when working online in the classroom. First, students ($N = 95$) asked via questionnaire about the effects of Internet use clearly identified this type of change when reporting how they felt when working on the Internet as compared to doing other kinds of classroom work. Specifically, students said that they felt more independent when working online. On a scale of 5 (feeling *much more independent*) to 1 (feeling *much less independent*), the mean response was 3.9, very near to 4.0 (*more independent*). Fewer than 2% of the students selected 2 (*less*) or 1 (*much less independent*). Students ($N = 94$) also

---

[2]Because different interviews were conducted annually and there were more participants in the NET every year, the number of individuals asked various questions and administered different questionnaires fluctuated depending on when a specific question was asked data gathering activity was undertaken.

reported experiencing a greater sense of control over their work online. (The overall mean was 3.8 on a 5-point scale, on which 4 indicated *more control*). The percentage of students reporting *less* or *much less control* (6%) was very small. Statistical tests showed no significant difference in the responses of elementary, middle and high school students.

The results from open-ended interviews with students and teachers are consistent with those just reported. Specifically, students commonly reported that teachers controlled and directed their work less when students worked online than otherwise. As one high school student put it:

> It's really like he [the teacher] acts different, because when he's teaching the class, it's sort of stuff we have to do, you know, assignments we have to do. But on the Internet, we have a lot more freedom to do almost whatever we want as long as we're getting the work done...

Younger students reported a similar phenomenon. For example, an elementary school student said:

> She lets us go free and see what we can learn about the Internet, and she doesn't let us go free when she's teaching the whole class.

Similarly, teachers reported that they were more likely to let students work autonomously on the Internet than otherwise. In fact, when asked a very general question about whether any changes in classroom roles or relationships resulted from Internet use, teachers were more likely to mention changes related to students' autonomy than almost any other category of response. As one high school teacher described it:

> Once you give them the assignment, and if you give them the addresses where they are to go and get the information, they work more independently. It requires less supervision. ...you become more of a facilitator, I would say, because...well, they get a chance to explore on their own.

Teachers' self-reports on a questionnaire, detailed information we collected about Internet-supported curricular projects, and classroom observations also support the conclusion that students engaged in Internet-supported activities often worked in a more autonomous manner than otherwise. For example, roughly 40% of teachers ($N = 83$) responding to a questionnaire about Internet use in the classroom reported that they provided help only when students requested it when students worked on Internet activities. Just 4% described themselves as presenting material to the students working on the Internet. (An additional 24% said that teachers and students work collaboratively to carry out Internet activities, and roughly 20% described themselves as guiding students through these activities via questions and comments.) And, in almost 60% of Internet curriculum projects that we tracked closely teachers described students as commonly functioning in an independent and self-directed manner.

The clear perceived increase in student control and autonomy related to Internet use is especially interesting in light of the fact that teachers commonly expressed concern about the possible negative consequences of student autonomy on the Internet and implemented procedures designed to control and circumscribe students' online activities. There were some educators who sought opportunities to increase student autonomy via use of the Internet, as will be discussed shortly. However, increasing student independence was not central to, or even initially desired by, many others. For example, in at least two of the annual competitions in which teams of teachers competed to join NET, the document explaining NET specifically indicated that a shift from a teacher-centered paradigm to a partnership model in which students had more control was highly desirable. Nonetheless, the large majority of the proposals submitted to the competition (80%) did not indicate that such a change was among the proposed projects' goals. Instead, proposals tended to emphasize other goals, such as preparing students' to live in an increasingly technological world (43%), expanding students' global awareness (37%), supporting interdisciplinary activities (35%), and increasing students' motivation (33%), all of which were mentioned noticeably more frequently than increasing their independence and control (20%).

Moreover, educators frequently implemented policies and practices specifically designed to direct and control students' behavior online (Schofield & Davidson, 2002). Such practices appeared to stem primarily from educators' concern about two factors—the consequences of students' encountering inappropriate material or potentially harmful individuals on-line and the potential for wasted time related to students' use of the Internet for noneducational purposes during school time. Even teachers desiring to further student autonomy set clear limits on the degree and kind of independence they wished to foster. For example, teachers were uniformly in agreement that they did not want students to access sexual materials from school, although some teachers were much more concerned about the potential consequences of students' exposure to such materials on the Internet than others. Furthermore, although there was less unanimity on this issue, even teachers who wished to use the Internet to foster increased student autonomy did not want students using class time for recreational activities. Yet, the tendency for students to do so, especially at the high school level, was strong. For example, when 42 high school students who had used the Internet for academic activities were asked whether and to what extent they drifted off task while working on-line during classroom time, 27 (64%) admitted unequivocally that they had done this. Of the 23 students specifying how often this occurred, 7 said they drifted from intended tasks every time they went on-line and another 8 said this happened with some frequency rather than infrequently. As one high school student described it:

> Brian: … sometimes—like when we were supposed to explore countries—…something might come up and you just don't want to leave it. You know, you want to keep looking into it and looking into it, and then you get off-task of what you're supposed to be doing. […] I'd say [that happens] about every time—every time.

This tendency to drift off to recreational sites is not limited to NET students, but has been noted in other school contexts as well (Thomas, 2000).

Concern about these two factors contributed to the emergence of numerous efforts to set limits on the autonomy that students had on the Internet. For example, policies and practices intended to prevent or minimize students' unsupervised access to the Internet in libraries or labs were common. Similarly, teachers adopted surveillance strategies including placing Internet-connected computers, so that their screens were readily visible to others and patrolling the classroom. Some educators even implemented specific curricular and technological strategies designed to allow them to direct students' on-line behavior along predetermined paths. For example, some teachers, especially those in elementary schools, created electronic bookmarks for the sites that their students were allowed to visit. One librarian required students to create a list of search terms that this educator would then approve ahead of time, while another instituted a keyboard checkout policy in order to check on students' intended use of the Internet before giving them access. Finally, an occasional educator resorted to using, or claiming to use, technical means to monitor the Internet sites students visited to help control student behavior.

There were also attempts to control the material that students presented to others over the Internet. For example, teachers sometimes previewed the e-mail students composed to make sure it did not contain content or language that the teachers felt were inappropriate. Teachers also monitored live chat to be sure that neither their students nor those with whom they were interacting strayed onto forbidden topics, such as sex, and there were controversies caused by high school students posting on personal home pages material to which teachers or administrators objected that was critical of their schools or teachers.

Ironically, in spite of the prevalence of educator behaviors designed to control students' on-line behavior, students still generally experienced more autonomy on-line than they otherwise did in their classes. We now turn to discussing the factors that contributed to this increase in students' sense of independence when using the Internet.

FACTORS CONTRIBUTING TO INCREASED STUDENT AUTONOMY AND CONTROL

Increased Access to External Resources

As previously mentioned, some NET teachers, especially those in high schools, wanted to provide students with increased autonomy and control over their work but had found it difficult to accomplish this goal to the extent that they desired before gaining Internet access. Such educators tended to see the Internet use as a means to enhance student independence. For example, as mentioned earlier, 20% of the educator teams participating in NET specifically expressed a desire in the proposals describing their curriculum projects to use Internet access to increase students' autonomy. Statements like the following, taken from a NET proposal, reveal such orientations: "Technology will make it possible for the teacher to be replaced, repositioned in the instructional scheme. Students will be increasingly self-directed."

Educators with this positive orientation toward increased student independence were better able to realize their visions with Internet access than without it for two reasons. First, access to the Internet could be used to give students the opportunity to interact with other adults, or even with knowledgeable peers. Thus, students' reliance on their classroom teacher was often significantly reduced. For example, teachers in one high school arranged for a small number of students to work with adult mentors. The teachers coached students in responding to challenges provided or questions asked by these mentors, but generally only when such help was requested since they were often not up to date on exactly where these interactions stood. In some instances, the teachers' traditional role as dispenser of knowledge was reversed since students interacted with experts in fields unfamiliar to the teacher and were able to attain copious information about their topics via Internet research or through Internet-facilitated interactions. This dynamic is at work in the following field note, taken in a high school chemistry classroom:

> [Mr. Jacobs, the teacher] had gotten an e-mail message from the ... doctor who LaToya had been working with on the research ...explaining in a very brief fashion what the research was about. He was having LaToya go over this message with him sentence by sentence to explain to him, because he said he

didn't understand what it all meant. He had her explain certain words, like there was some kind of che-motherapy drug that she had to explain. [She also] explained the main function of the drug, which was to retard the growth of the cancer cells ... by cutting the DNA so that the cells could not reproduce. Mr. Jacobs also had her draw a picture of what this particular cell ... looked like.

A second reason that educators who wished to enhance student independence were able to better realize this goal with Internet access was that it was possible for students to use the Internet to find information for themselves that teachers would otherwise have felt obliged to provide. This, in turn, allowed teachers to place the burden for education more directly on their students and often enhanced students' independence. For example, a foreign language teacher indicated that with the advent of classroom Internet access he let students begin to construct their own vo-cabulary lists from materials they encountered at foreign language sites rather than supplying them with lists of words to learn as he had previously. An elementary school teacher said, when asked if having the Internet had changed the way she did lesson-planning:

Ms. DeLuca: We have a whole different viewpoint on ... curriculum (now)... The kids are in charge of the curriculum ... Like take a topic like Native Americans. They are in charge of the learning. They ask the questions ... They have to find the resources, and they find the answers to the questions any way that it takes.

WHOLE CLASS INSTRUCTION COMBINED WITH A HIGH STUDENT/COMPUTER RATIO

Although, as discussed previously, some teachers intentionally used the ready access to external resources provided by the Internet to increase student independence, this goal was not central to, or even initially desired by, many others. Nonetheless, as indicated earlier, a shift toward somewhat increased levels of perceived student independence and control was widely evident in NET class-rooms. Here, we discuss two factors that combined to limit teachers' ability to guide and control students during Internet-based activities and to support autonomy even when such changes were not actively planned or desired by teachers. The first was the prevalence in NET classrooms, espe-cially at the middle and high school levels, of whole class instructional methods. The second was that NET teams tended to distribute the Internet-connected computers they received relatively evenly among the classrooms of participating teachers, rather than placing them in a central labora-tory. This resulted in a relatively high student/computer ratio in most NET classrooms. Indeed it was common for NET classrooms to have no more than one to three or four computers.

Educators working in classrooms with a high student/computer ratio frequently tended to have individual students or small groups of students work on-line independently while the teacher guided the large majority of the class's students through other activities as a group. This let teach-ers proceed essentially as usual with their typical teaching practices while simultaneously allow-ing them to let some students make use of the Internet. Teachers in this kind of situation were typically fully occupied with their whole class instruction. Thus, they generally did not have much time to supervise the small subset of students working on the Internet. In fact, some teachers found trying to juggle both activities so difficult that they made special arrangements with their col-leagues in order to avoid being pulled in too many directions at once, as indicated by the following conversation occurring between elementary school teachers at a NET team meeting:

Ms. Fisher ... pointed to ... where Ms. Nacarato had written," ... I found it difficult to work [on the Internet] with a student or group while conducting class." Ms. Fisher pointed this out to Ms. Gerard [who] immediately said, "Yes ..."[Ms. Gerard then explained how she and another teacher double-up so that one of them can pull a small number of students out of class to work with her ... on the Internet ... while the other teaches an unusually large group in her normal manner. Next, she said,] "You know, I really think it would be too difficult to do it [use the Internet in class] otherwise."

Most teachers in classes with small numbers of computers did not make such special arrangements. Thus, they almost *had* to allow students using the Internet while their classmates participated in whole class instruction to work more independently than usual. Otherwise, the teacher was forced to spend significantly less time than usual supervising the whole classroom or to undertake the daunting task of teaching "two classes at once," as one teacher put it. Indeed, as a consequence of the many demands on their time in such situations, teachers often specifically asked students working on the Internet to rely, if possible, on themselves or their peers for assistance when difficulties arose, thus clearly increasing students' independence.

TECHNICAL STRUCTURE OF THE INTERNET

Even in lab environments in which large numbers of students could access the Internet simultaneously, students using the Internet still tended to work more autonomously than they did when not using the Internet. This is due to the fact that, for a variety of reasons, the Internet lends itself more readily to individualized sorts of instructional tasks and outcomes than to whole group activities. First, because the World Wide Web has a hypertextual structure students engaged in similar Internet-based searches often ended up in extremely different places, and their paths diverged very quickly. Teachers often asked students to carry out searches on a given topic. However, unless teachers required all students to use the Internet in an absolutely uniform way—that is, to use precisely the same search engine and search terms, to visit the same web sites, and to collect exactly the same information—students typically made many decisions about what information to get, experienced different challenges along the way, and arrived at very different end points. Although there would clearly also be some degree of variation if students in a class were all asked to gather information on a given topic from their texts or from books in the classroom library, the range of information available on the Internet is certainly larger than that contained in the other resources in most classrooms and the choice points students encounter are likely to be much more numerous.

Furthermore, reflecting its history, the Internet is structured for individual exploratory work rather than for identical work by large numbers of people simultaneously (Davidson, Schofield, & Stocks, 2001). So, when teachers who had access to a laboratory attempted to direct and control student activity by having all students do the same thing on-line at the same time significant problems arose. Specifically, the web sites to which they intended their students to go often became overloaded, resulting in very slow access or in denials of entry to at least some students due to heavy traffic. These factors combined to make individually-oriented tasks more attractive to teachers, which made it easier for students to have some input, and led to teachers working in a troubleshooting capacity rather than in a strongly directive way. Consequently, students using the Internet often found themselves working more independently of their teacher than otherwise, as indicated by the following comments of a high school teacher:

Mr. Galbraith: The (Internet-based) research class, if you go in and look at the Web pages from last year, they ... the students specifically said, "We learned more from each other than we learned from Mr. Galbraith or Mr. Waleska," ... And the point is, when you have two teachers and 25 kids and they're all working at the keyboards, you can't spend the whole period with every student. And if one kid knows how to do it, they show each other. [...] I will show two or three kids, because they're ready to learn it at that point, and by the time we get through the class, the rest of the class already knows this because they've passed on ... they've been teaching each other.

REVERSAL OF THE USUAL TEACHER STUDENT KNOWLEDGE DISPARITY

Another factor that strongly contributed to students' increased independence was that it was common for students to know as much or more about the Internet as their teachers. NET teachers were neither highly proficient computer users nor deeply knowledgeable about the Internet and all it has to offer. For example, a full 89% of the teachers attending an Internet training course in which all NET educators were expected to enroll reported that they had little or no experience with the Internet before their participation in NET. Similarly, about two–thirds of the educators replying to a survey in NET's 4th year ($N = 323$) reported that they were Internet novices at NET's inception. Students, especially at the high school level, often said that they knew more about the Internet than their teachers, a claim with which their teachers and observers tended to agree. Students were far less likely to give this sort of answer when asked whether they knew more about the classroom subject material than their teachers. (For more details regarding teachers' level of familiarity with the Internet see Schofield, Davidson, Stocks, & Futoran, 1997 or Schofield & Davidson, 2002.)

The reversal of the usual knowledge disparity between teachers and students tended to increase student independence because it led teachers to encourage students who were proficient Internet users to help other students using the Internet when they were so inclined. Teachers did so not only because they wanted extra help, but also in some instances because they were aware that some students were more likely to be able to solve a problem than they were. This meant that such students were able to decide when and if they would leave their seats, talk with other students, and turn away from teacher-assigned activities—behaviors that teachers very often attempt to control otherwise. Indeed, a few high school students, who were highly skilled Internet users, moved beyond such activities and even began to function as technical experts, taking on substantial responsibility for managing and maintaining their schools' servers and computers and performing jobs their teachers were not knowledgeable enough to undertake. This role gave them a striking degree of control and independence since they had access to an important and expensive school resource that often contained various sorts of confidential information. Further, they had such access in a context in which the adults in the school were often not able to direct or control their behavior very effectively, because of a lack of understanding of the technical issues.

Students' greater ease and familiarity with the Internet occasionally contributed to increasing their control over their work in yet another way. Students sometimes identified web sites that they thought complemented a given theme or topic being addressed in the classroom, alerted the teacher to their existence and location, and ended up influencing what they and their classmates did. For example, one high school teacher recalled:

> Students went out and found diagrams for physics demonstrations in electrostatic, printed the demonstration, came back and said, "Can we do this? Do we have the equipment? I didn't know we could do this kind of stuff. Help me understand what is going on here." So the Internet has acted to stimulate, actually, what is going on in class.

In principal, students could also contribute to the curriculum by calling teachers' attention to materials found in newspapers, magazines, or in other sources. But, we rarely if ever saw this happen, perhaps at least partly because the teachers were, generally speaking, likely to be at least as familiar with such sources as students. Also, students' strong interest in and desire to use the Internet, discussed at length in Schofield and Davidson (2002), most likely contributed to their tendency to suggest the use of materials found there.

WARMER LESS ADVERSARIAL
TEACHER–STUDENT RELATIONSHIPS

A second change in classroom roles and relationships related to Internet use concerns the quality of day-to-day interactions between teachers and their students. Specifically, both teachers and students reported that their relationships tended to be warmer and less adversarial during Internet activities than at other times. For example, students routinely reported during interviews that, when using the Internet, teachers acted happier, treated the class more "nicely," and tended to yell less than otherwise. And, when given a questionnaire asking them to compare how friendly their teachers seemed when students were working on Internet activities compared to other times in the classroom, students ($N = 92$) indicated that their teachers were more friendly in the Internet situation. Elementary school students were especially likely to report a change in this regard. Indeed, of those students, 73.1% indicated that their teacher seemed more or much more friendly when the Internet was being used, and this group's mean response on a five-point scale, on which 4 represented *more friendly*, was 4.1. Many students at the middle and the high school levels gave this sort of response as well, with means of 3.5 and 3.3 respectively on the same 5-point scale. Only a very small percentage of any age group reported that teachers were less or much less friendly when using the Internet.

Similarly, and consistent with student reports, many teachers reported that their relationships with students were positively affected by Internet use. Comments like the one below from a NET educator illustrate this perspective:

> Ms. Ebert: You're much closer to the kids you've worked with on the Net, because you get to do them in a small group. And not only that, when they start commenting about stories, or when they have e-mail with somebody, you start learning how they feel as people ... it makes them like ... they're more of a little human being, and you're more of a real human being to them.

This change in the affective quality of student–teacher relationships is especially interesting because, although it seemed quite widespread, it did not appear to be at all planned. For example, to analyze the funded projects' stated goals a coding system was constructed based on the goals commonly mentioned in NET proposals. Of the roughly 20 data-based categories included in the coding system, such as providing a broader audience for students' work, enhancing student motivation, and increasing students' independence, not a single category reflected a desire to improve student–teacher relationships because this goal was so infrequently mentioned. Furthermore, interviews with teachers regarding what they hoped to accomplish with NET and how they would judge success also suggested that such outcomes were rarely, if ever, sought. Next we discuss the ways in which Internet use appeared to foster positive teacher–student relationships.

FACTORS CONTRIBUTING TO MORE POSITIVE
TEACHER–STUDENT RELATIONSHIPS

More Private and Personal Context for Teacher–Student Interaction

Much of the unintended positive change in student–teacher relationships appeared to stem from that fact that when using the Internet students worked more often in small groups than they did otherwise. As one teacher put it, reflecting on how Internet use had changed her class, "I'm not doing so much large group teaching (anymore)." Working in a more private, personalized and individual context led to improved student–teacher relationships in a number of ways. Specifically, it gave teachers an opportunity to connect more directly with their students about topics of personal interest to the students as well as about academic matters, since teachers could tailor their comments more readily to specific students' concerns. In addition, in these sorts of relatively private situations teachers could communicate more effectively with students who tended not to speak up otherwise. As one elementary school teacher observed when discussing how Internet use changed her relationship with students:

> Ms. Gerard: I mean, I always try to listen to them, but…it seems that they're more willing to say things and tell their little stories when it's a smaller group. It's more intimate. Maybe it's more comfortable for them for whatever reason […] For instance, Derrik you may notice is very quiet. He doesn't tend to be a real talker, and he's very quiet in class. He'll raise his hand and answer questions, but in working with him on the Internet, we have…I've heard things about his parents and his trips that I don't think I would have heard in a large group.

In short, removed from the public spotlight of the classroom, students spoke up more readily and teachers saw them more distinctly and individually. In addition, in these individualized or small group interchanges teachers did not have to raise their voices to get students' attention and the criticism they directed to students was not apparent to the entire class. Therefore, even when individuals deviated from their teacher's agenda while using the Internet, there was generally little need for the kind of public contest of wills that can polarize the situation and worsen teacher–student relationships.

Teachers not only had the opportunity to get to know their students better in the individualized interactions and the small group situations fostered by Internet use, but students came to know and appreciate their teachers better as individuals via Internet-related interactions. Some teachers revealed personal feelings, perspectives, or vulnerabilities during encounters with individual students or small groups of students working on the Internet more than they did otherwise in whole class situations. Also, their uncertainties and difficulties relating to technology were often quite apparent. Therefore, they may have looked more human; like individuals also struggling with the task of learning. In the following field note, for example, elementary school students see their teacher as a feeling individual as they empathize with her about a problem encountered as she tried to move e-mail from one file to another.

> The room was incredibly loud at this moment, and suddenly in the midst of it, Ms. Ebert exclaimed, "Oh, this is not my day!" Danielle turned sharply towards Mike and said, "Don't yell! She's having a hard time. She might erase everything." Ms. Ebert was kneeling on the floor with her elbows on the table that the computers were sitting on, and she hung her head and ran her fingers through her hair. It turned out she had erased, or she believed that she had erased, all of the letters that she had highlighted instead of moving them. She said a couple of times, "I just can't believe this. I can't believe this." Danielle began to pat her back soothingly, as if to reassure her.

In addition to helping students see their teachers as individuals who, like students, experience frustration, moments like these can help build camaraderie for two reasons. First, both teachers and students noted that students can identify a point of similarity between themselves and the adult in such situations. This has implications for teacher–student relations because increased perceptions of similarity commonly lead to increased liking (Berscheid & Reis, 1998). Second, as discussed shortly, such situations provide an opportunity for students to help teachers, an experience they typically found gratifying.

TEACHERS' ENHANCED APPRECIATION
OF STUDENTS' CAPABILITIES

Some teachers, especially those in high schools, reported that they developed a more multifaceted and appreciative view of some youths' potential when working with them on Internet-based activities. Sometimes students who had not impressed teachers greatly in other classroom activities evidenced unexpected skill at Internet use, which changed teachers' perceptions of them in ways that were likely to be gratifying to the students. These sorts of occurrences are illustrated in the quotes below, both from high school teachers:

> Mr. Jacobs: Kids that I wouldn't think were academically gifted are gifted on the Internet and ... surprise me by what they've been able to do.
>
> Ms. Hoffman: Well, it (Internet use) enabled me to see some of my students in a different light. Some who were very capable in language skills were quite uncomfortable with the computer. And, on the other hand, those who struggled with language may have had an opportunity to really shine because they were more comfortable with the Internet than they were with their language ...

In many cases, both those in which teachers had an initially high opinion of a student and those in which they did not, teachers made good use of students' technical skills in interactions that appeared to help build positive bonds between them. As one high school teacher put it, reflecting on the positive consequences of working along side of knowledgeable students to solve technical problems:

Ms. Richardson: ... it breaks down barriers there for both of us, because they know so much more than I do, sometimes, and other times, I can help them along. So, it puts you on the same level. You're both learners. It's not like, they're looking to you to give all the answers, and I think it really helps to achieve a nice bridge in learning. You just, you feel comfortable together, or frustrated together, as well.

Consistent with the preceding, students with strong technical skills who helped their teachers learn how to use the Internet effectively talked in very positive ways about the impact of these interactions on teacher–student relationships. For example, a high school student who helped her teacher learn various basic Internet skills spoke positively about being treated as an equal, rather than as a child, by her teacher and of enjoying the experience:

Shamara: When I was ... on the Internet ... the computer froze, and she [the teacher] did not know what was going on so we had to tell her. And she didn't know how to print ... and I guess got nervous or something, so we just had to show her ... She was ... surprised.
Interviewer: ... Did she treat you differently?
Shamara: Yeah ... She like treated (us) like we was (sic) equal, not one is adult and one is a child ... like equal.
Interviewer: And how did that make you feel?
Shamara: Good ... like finally somebody's treating me like I'm the same as them, not a little kid.

INCREASED STUDENT ENJOYMENT AND MOTIVATION

Enhanced enjoyment and increased motivation for students were outcomes linked to Internet use across all age levels that we studied. (See Schofield & Davidson [2002] for a more detailed discussion of this finding.) For example, in response to one close-ended question about how much fun Internet use was compared to other classroom activities, 83% of the students responding ($N = 72$) selected one of the two positive options indicating that the Internet was *more fun* or *much more fun* than other classroom activities. In striking contrast, only 3% selected one of the two options indicating that it was *less fun* or *much less fun*. Not only did students appear to enjoy class more when using the Internet, they also consistently reported feeling more motivated. For example, among students from all school levels whom we interviewed on this topic ($N = 73$), 50% reported finding it easier to concentrate while using the Internet than at other times in class. Only 5% reported that it was harder to concentrate.

Teachers clearly noticed students' increased levels of enjoyment and motivation. Notably, 80% of the teachers ($N = 56$) asked in interviews to characterize the reactions of their students to Internet use reported generally positive responses. In sharp contrast, not a single teacher reported generally negative responses. Indeed, consistent with other research suggesting that Internet use motivates students (Neilsen, 1998; Songer, 1996), some teachers, all at the high school level, reported that Internet use actually motivated students to arrive on class on time, to attend classes that they would otherwise have cut, or to start work on projects well in advance rather than putting them off to the last minute.

When students tackle their work readily and engage less in disrespectful or disruptive behavior, such as arriving late for class, teachers have more time to interact with them in positive ways, more energy to expend on personalizing teacher–student relationships, and less reason to resent or criticize their behaviors. Not surprisingly, such changes improve teacher–student relations. In addition, seeing students respond positively to school work led to a positive reaction in teachers, which may account for students' observation that their teachers appeared generally more positive and happy when students engaged in on-line activities than otherwise. The following comment from a high school teacher is consistent with this conclusion:

> Ms. Richardson: Some teachers, it's (Internet use) given them a renewed sense of what they're here for and how they can relate to kids and that they have something new to give to kids [...] You suddenly learn that if kids are gonna respond to something in this manner and you're good at it, then you're gonna have a better time with the kids.

INCREASED AUTONOMY

As discussed previously, there was strong evidence that Internet use tended to enhance student autonomy. Interesting, this change was not only important in and of itself. It had implications for the quality of teacher–student relationships in both a direct and an indirect way. At a period in their lives when they were engaged in the process of forging individual identities, students, especially at the middle and high school level, sometimes chaffed at school rules and resented at least mildly teachers' attempts to control and direct many aspects of their personal and academic behavior. The increase in autonomy that frequently accompanied Internet use mitigated this source of friction between students and teachers and thus contributed directly to improving their relationships. In addition, students quite commonly took advantage of their relatively high levels of autonomy on the Internet to explore, at least briefly, entertainment or recreational web. This did not generally appear to be constructive from an educational perspective. However, it was often less disruptive to the class than were many of the other ways that students sought relief when bored or tired. Indeed, it was so unobtrusive that teachers were often unaware of the fact that a student had strayed to such sites, and thus were not annoyed by it. In contrast, other behaviors that students commonly used to mitigate boredom or to fill empty moments, such as socializing with peers, were often quite obvious and potentially disruptive, characteristics that made them more likely to create friction between teacher and students,

With regard to the indirect impact of increased autonomy on teacher–student relationships, one of the reasons students gave for the increased enjoyment and motivation they experienced with Internet use, which played an important role in improving teacher–student relations as discussed above, was the increased autonomy they often experienced when using the Internet. Thus, increased autonomy not only improved teacher–student relationships in some quite direct ways, it also did so more indirectly, through its impact on enjoyment and motivation. For example, students often took advantage to the autonomy they had when using the Internet to connect their schoolwork more closely with their personal interests than they were able to do otherwise, something that they typically enjoyed and found motivating. This increased enjoyment and motivation improved student–teacher relations in ways described earlier.

DISCUSSION AND CONCLUSIONS

Like numerous other computer applications, the Internet has the potential to change classrooms as teachers intend as well as to change them in potentially important although unplanned ways. Specifically, our findings suggest that in an urban United States context, Internet use tends to increase students' autonomy and control over their work, both in the classrooms of teachers who wished to use the Internet to foster this change and in classrooms in which such a change was not foreseen or initially desired. This study also suggests that Internet use frequently encourages the development of warmer less adversarial student–teacher relationships, an outcome that was almost never anticipated. These changes were experienced by students in elementary, middle, and high schools, as well, as by students of both European–American and African–American ancestry.

The particular changes occurring in conjunction with Internet use in NET classrooms seem generally positive in nature. Specifically, research discussed earlier in this article suggests that in the United States context increased student independence may well have positive consequences. Consistent with this we observed many cases in which increased autonomy in the classroom seemed to facilitate learning on the part of students. For example, students given responsibility for supporting Internet use in their school or for helping their peers use the Internet often leaned a great deal in the process of doing so quite independently of their teachers. Further, in a smaller number of cases, students took advantage of their autonomy to participate in Internet-mediated interactions with mentors whose specialized expertise supported their learning in ways their teachers could not. In addition, there is reason to think that warmer student–teacher relations are valuable. Teachers and students in this study spoke very positively about this change and its consequences. And, as discussed earlier, prior research also suggests such a change is likely to be desirable in a number of respects. For example, Hawkins (1993) suggested that students learn well when they are in environment in which they are personally well known, an outcome that seems very likely to be closely linked to the quality of student–teacher relations.

However, it is important to recognize that changes accompanying Internet use in the classroom, whether planned or unplanned, can have down sides to them as well. For example, although most students were quite enthusiastic about opportunities for increased autonomy and many teachers valued this change as well, occasionally students reported frustration associated with this increased independence in circumstance when they felt they did not get the support they needed from teachers. Further, we observed numerous instances in which students working autonomously on the Internet would clearly have benefited from a teacher's assistance either in solving a specific problem or in learning how to solve the general class of problem they faced. For example, one student spent 20 minutes unsuccessfully searching the Internet for material for a paper because she misspelled the word, Asia, that she used as a search term. Advice on the correct spelling of the word, on how to handle the problem when searches that should yield material do not, and on how to frame searches so that they are not overly broad would all most likely have facilitated her learning. Without such support she did not move forward.

In addition, although many students were able to make good use of their increased independence, a substantial portion of them used the increased autonomy they experienced when using the Internet to spend time that was intended to further their education playing games, visiting entertainment sites of questionable educational valuable, and even, for some, veering off into locating materials that most would consider inappropriate for student consumption (Schofield & Davidson, 2002). Thus, increased student autonomy is not an unmitigated good. Its impact most likely depends on factors such as whether it occurs in an environment that provides reasonably prompt and effective support when the student hits an impasse and the degree to which the environment provides temptations that students will have a hard time resisting.

Of course, Internet use is far from the only way, and might not even be the most effective or efficient way, to bring about the changes in student–teacher relationships discussed in this article. Other changes in classroom artifacts, practices, or activities might well do the same. That having been said, it is important to remember that teachers respond most positively to changes that they believe will further their goals and help them solve problems they see as important (Cuban, 1986). Few NET teachers indicated that increasing student independence or improving student–teacher relations were high-priority for them. Thus, it is rather unrealistic to think that artifacts, practices, or activities specifically designed to foster such outcomes would be widely and enthusiastically welcomed.

In sum, this article emphasizes the importance of recognizing that Internet use may well bring about unplanned as well as planned changes in the social functioning of the classroom. Furthermore, it suggests that such changes can importantly change the environment in which students learn in both direct and in more indirect ways.

ACKNOWLEDGMENTS

The research reported here, was funded by Contract No. RED–9253452 with the National Science Foundation, Grant No. 42–40–94032 from the United States Department of Commerce, and Grant No. 199800209 from the Spencer Foundation. All opinions expressed herein are solely those of the authors and no endorsement of the conclusions by the National Science Foundation, the U.S. Department of Commerce, or the Spencer Foundation is implied or intended.

REFERENCES

Ames, C. A. (1990). Motivation: What teachers need to know. *Teachers College Record, 91,* 410–414.

Berscheid, E., & Reis, H. T. (1998). Attraction and close relationships. In D. T. Gilbert, S. T. Fiske, & G. Lindzey (Eds.), *The handbook of social psychology* (4th ed., Vol. 1, pp. 193–281). New York: McGraw-Hill.

Cuban, L. (1986). *Teachers and machines: The classroom use of technology since 1920.* New York: Teachers College Press.

Davidson, A. L. (1999). Negotiating social differences: Youths' assessments of educators' strategies. *Urban Education, 34,* 338–369.

Davidson, A. L., Schofield, J. W., & Stocks, J. E. (2001). Professional cultures and collaborative efforts: A case study of technologists and educators working for change. *The Information Society, 17,* pp. 21–32.

Goodlad, J. I. (1984). *A place called school.* New York: McGraw-Hill.

Greenfield, P. M. (1994). Independence and interdependence as developmental scripts: Implications for theory, research and practice. In P. M. Greenfield & R. R. Cocking (Eds.), *Cross-cultural roots of minority child development* (pp. 1–40). Hillsdale, NJ: Lawrence Erlbaum Associates, Inc.

Hativa, N. (1994). What you design is not what you get (WYDINWYG): Cognitive, affective, and social impacts of learning with ILS – an integration of findings from six-years of qualitative and quantitative studies. *International Journal of Educational Research, 21,* 81–112.

Hawkins, J. (1984, April). *Paired problem solving in a computer context.* Paper presented at the meeting of the American Educational Research Association, New Orleans, LA.

Hawkins, J. (1987). The interpretation of Logo in practice. In R. D. Pea & K. Sheingold (Eds.), *Mirrors of minds: Patterns of experience in educational computing* (pp. 3–34). Stamford, CT: Ablex.

Hawkins, J. (1993). *Technology and the organization of schooling* (Tech. Rep. No. 28). New York: Center for Technology in Education.

Heath, S. B. (1993). *Ways with words: Language, life and work in communities and classrooms.* Cambridge: Cambridge University Press.

Henderson, V. L., & Dweck, C. S. (1990). Motivation and achievement. In S. S. Feldman & G. R. Elliott (Eds.), *At the threshold: The developing adolescent* (pp. 308–329). Cambridge, MA: Harvard University Press.

Kling, R. (1996). Computerization at work. In R. Kling (Ed.), *Computerization and controversy: Value conflicts and social choices* (2nd ed., pp. 1–34). San Diego, CA: Academic.

Kvale, S. (1996). *InterViews: An introduction to qualitative research interviewing.* Thousand Oaks, CA: Sage.

Lebra, T. S. (1994). Mother and child in Japanese socialization: A Japan-U.S. comparison. In P. M. Greenfield & R. R. Cocking (Eds.), *Cross-cultural roots of minority child development* (pp. 259–274). Mahwah, NJ: Lawrence Erlbaum Associates, Inc.

Lortie, D. C. (1975). *School teacher: A sociological study.* Chicago: University of Chicago Press.

Mantovani, G., & Spagnolli, A. (2000). Imagination and culture: What is it like being in the cyberspace? *Mind, Culture and Activity, 7,* 217–226.

Neilsen, L. (1998). Coding the light: Rethinking generational authority in a rural high school telecommunications project. In D. Reinking, M.C. McKenna, L. D. Labbo, & R. D. Kieffer (Eds.), *Handbook of literacy and technology: Transformations in a post- typographic world.* Mahwah, NJ: Lawrence Erlbaum Associates, Inc.

Olson, S. (1976). *Ideas and data: Process and practice of social research.* Homewood, IL: Dorsey.

Ravitz, J. S., Becker, H. J., & Wong, Y. T. (2000, July). Constructivist-compatible beliefs and practices among United States' teachers. *Teaching, Learning, and Computing: 1998 National Survey* (Report #4). University of California, Irvine and University of Minnesota: Center for Research on Information Technology and Organizations. Retrieved February, 14, 2003 from http://www.crito.uci.edu/tlc/html/findings.html

Roeser, R. W., Midgley, C., & Urdan, T. (1996). Perceptions of the school psychological environment and early adolescents' psychological and behavioral functioning in school: The mediating role of goals and belonging. *Journal of Educational Psychology 88*(3), 408–422.

Schofield, J. W. (1995). *Computers and classroom culture.* New York: Cambridge University Press.

Schofield, J. W. (1997, Spring). Computers and classroom social processes: A review of the literature. *Social Science Computer Review, 15*(1), 27–39.

Schofield, J. W., & Davidson, A. L. (2002). *Bringing the Internet to school: Lessons learned from an urban district.* San Francisco: Jossey-Bass.

Schofield, J. W., Davidson, A. L., Stocks, J. E., & Futoran, G. (1997). The Internet in school: A case study of educators' demand and its precursors. In S. Kiesler (Ed.), *Culture of the Internet* (pp. 361–381). Mahwah, NJ: Lawrence Erlbaum Associates, Inc.

Sheingold, K., Hawkins, J., & Char, C. (1984). The interaction of technology and the social life of classrooms. *Journal of Social Issues, 40*(3), 49–61.

Songer, N. B. (1996). Exploring learning opportunities in coordinated network enhanced classrooms: A case of kids as global scientists. *The Journal of the Learning Sciences, 5,* 297–328.

Spindler, G., & Spindler, L. (1987). In prospect for a controlled cross-cultural comparison of schooling: Schoenhausen and Roseville. In G. D. Spindler (Ed.), *Education and cultural process: Anthropological approaches* (2nd ed., pp. 389–400). Prospect Heights, IL: Waveland Press.

Tharp, R. G., & Gallimore, R. (1991). *Rousing minds to life: Teaching, learning, and schooling in social context.* Cambridge: Cambridge University Press.

Thomas, K. (2000, February 17). Online school kids search, play all day: Educational sites given short shrift by students. *USA Today,* p. 3D . Retrieved February, 14, 2003, from http://pqasb.pqarchiver.com/USAToday/main/doc/

Wehlage, G. G., & Rutter, R. A. (1986). Dropping out: How much do schools contribute to the problem? *Teachers College Record, 87,* 374–392.

Wentzel, K. R. (1998). Social relationships and motivation in middle school: The role of parents, teachers and peers. *Journal of Educational Psychology, 90,* 202–209.

Wentzel, K. R., & Wigfield, A. (1998). Academic and social motivational influences on students' academic performance. *Educational Psychology Review, 10,* 155–175.

MIND, CULTURE, AND ACTIVITY, *10*(1), 80–85

Some Special Features of This Special Issue: Core Values and Possible Next Steps

John Bransford

Learning Technology Center
Peabody College
Vanderbilt University

The articles in this special issue provide insightful analyses of people's interactions as mediated by artifacts such as computers, the Internet, and more traditional structures such as gardens and houses. These artifacts are never "culturally neutral"; the authors do an excellent job of highlighting the (often unexpected) changes in roles, responsibilities and beliefs that arise when new artifacts are introduced.

My primary goal is to explore some features that all the articles appear to have in common. I was particularly struck by the "stance" toward research exemplified by each of the authors—a stance that is very different from many approaches to the study of culture and technology. For example, read (or re- read) the description of early cross-cultural research that Michael Cole (1996) described in the beginning chapters of his book. He summarized a number of studies where researchers had attempted to measure the ability of people from other cultures to engage in supposedly "culturally neutral" and "intelligent" activities such as reasoning, remembering, problem solving and concept formation. More often than not the people being studied fell short by the researchers' standards. As Cole emphasized however, it is ultimately the researchers who fell short in terms of understanding the multiple ways that people can "be smart."

Thinking about the contrast between early cultural research and the present articles prompted me to organize my remarks around a concept that I call "The Jan Perspective." The Jan Perspective reflects a set of core values that are extremely important for research and practice, including efforts to understand and harness the potentials of new technologies. These core values include the following assumptions:

• What counts most is the quality of life of people. Academic knowledge and skills (in mathematics, science, etc.) can enhance the quality of peoples' lives; so can economic assets. Ultimately, however, particular sets of knowledge, skills and economic assets should be seen as means toward something more important—not as ends in and of themselves.
• There are valuable lessons to be learned from every person and group, but these lessons will become apparent only if you approach interactions with genuine respect, and if you take the time

Requests for reprints should be sent to John Bransford, Learning Technology Center, Peabody College, Box 45, Vanderbilt University, Nashville, TN 37203. E-mail: john.bransford@vanderbilt.edu

to observe and listen rather than fall prey to the common tendency to talk too much and to judge everything based on your existing point of view.

• Breakthrough learning requires the courage to enter situations that disrupt our typical comfort zones. Experiencing these new settings helps make tacit knowledge more explicit; it leads to insights about our beliefs and cultural practices that would probably remain hidden otherwise.

• Artifacts are never "culturally neutral" and researchers should not view them as "fixed entities" that can simply be inserted into different cultural contexts which are then treated as independent variables. Instead, artifacts are catalysts for new kinds of human interactions—many of which cannot be predicted ahead of time.

Certainly Jan Hawkins is not the only person in the world who reflects these kinds of values. In fact, she did her doctoral studies with Michael Cole and members of his laboratory, and these are the kinds of values that they emphasized. I'm still going to call this "The Jan Perspective" because she is an outstanding example of a larger community of scholars who live by these values and "walk the walk" rather than simply "talk the talk." When I refer to the Jan Perspective, I hope readers will understand that it represents my deep and enduring respect for Jan, and that I see her as an example of a larger group of researchers who take a stance toward research that has powerful implications for what is studied, how it is studied, and how interpretations are made.

BUILDING HOUSES, BUILDING LIVES

The article by Lorie Hammond fits the Jan Perspective very strongly. It provides a fascinating account of a project where mainstream teachers worked with a group of Iu Mienh immigrants (from a Laotian hill tribe) on a school community garden project. The teachers and the parents collaborated with children to build a garden and a Iu Mienh field house at an urban school, and to write stories about their work. Hammond's descriptions of the interactions that occurred are fascinating.

This approach to "immigrant education" contrasts sharply with many others. For example, I suspect we all know of cases where attempts to help new immigrants adapt to US school systems involves "experts" telling the "newcomers" how to be successful. Often the communication is totally one-sided. The newcomers are the naive recipients and the "experts" are in power and in charge.

The project described by Hammond represents a distinct alternative to one-sided "power and privilege" relationships. It explicitly assumes that members of both participating cultures have something to contribute and something to learn from one another. It expects issues to emerge that were not predicted beforehand and hence can cause a little chaos—in short, the project requires the courage to risk shake-ups of normal routines of living. Overall, the core values reflected in The Jan Perspective are present throughout the entire project that Hammond describes.

It seems clear that Hammond is not proposing that Iu Mienh houses, or other kinds of houses, should be built in every community in the country. Instead, she documents the value of creating opportunities for transcultural communication, adaptation and learning, and her arguments fit squarely with The Jan Perspective. Without this perspective, efforts to build houses or create garden projects would probably produce outcomes that fall far short of those that Hammond so wonderfully describes.

TOWARD A FRAMEWORK FOR CULTURALLY RESPONSIVE DESIGN

In both her articles for this volume and on numerous other situations (e.g., EdTalk.org), Carol Lee has helped me appreciate how communities of practice that exist outside of school are often not connected to in-school learning. We know that all new learning is strongly affected by previous learning (see, e.g., Bransford, Brown & Cocking, 1999—especially chap. 3). If we fail to help students make connections between school-based learning and out-of-school practices (practices that often reflect highly sophisticated competencies yet frequently are not recognized as such), we are severely limiting their chances for success. In addition, by celebrating nontraditional competencies ("nontraditional" from the perspective of formal schooling), we become much more aligned with The Jan Perspective which helps equalize "power and privilege" relationships by assuming that all people have something to teach as well as learn.

Carol Lee focuses on ways that educational technology can—but usually does not—fit principles of "culturally responsive design." I very much like this name because it fits perfectly with the Jan Perspective and leads to a number of very important issues that Lee correctly notes have tended to be ignored in the literature. For example, one way to be culturally unresponsive is to force all students into a single "lock step" (conveyor belt) instructional program that purports to be "culturally neutral" (but isn't). Unfortunately, this situation exists in many schools.

Ideally, culturally responsive designs will allow different students to build on different strengths, such as funds of knowledge available in their homes and community. On the other hand, it is doubtful that we want each group of students to essentially have their own curriculum and never interact. We need opportunities for shared interactions and emergent insights like those that are so nicely illustrated in the present issue. One possibility is to search for artifacts that consistently capture peoples' imaginations even though they do not necessarily map directly into their life experiences. For example, movies like Star Wars seem to have pretty universal appeal to children. So do certain science and literary activities. The important point is that there may be several routes to being "culturally responsive." One is to map into familiar settings; the other is to capture students' imaginations by creating new settings that have strong appeal. My reading of Lee's article is that she includes examples of both of these.

Lee also makes a comment (in the implications section of her article) that I appreciate greatly and take very seriously. While arguing that computer based environments that support learning must take issues of culture into account, she notes:

"… the discipline of Black Psychology has addressed such issues for almost 30 years (Boykin, 1994; McAdoo & McAdoo, 1985; Nobles, 1980). However, unfortunately, the dominant literature in the cognitive sciences acts as though this body of research simply doesn't exist."

I must admit that I do not know these studies as well as I should, and I am eager to accept Lee's invitation to explore them in more detail. One of the major reasons is that there are "power and privilege" relationship that can be totally invisible to some people (e.g., members of a majority culture in a society) yet starkly (often painfully) visible to others. By drawing on the life experiences of many different groups, we can get a much clear picture of how societies work and how they might be improved.

THE INTERNET AS A SOURCE OF UNINTENDED CLASSROOM CHANGE

Schofield and Davidson discuss some of the lessons from their study of a large urban school district that brought Internet access to classrooms. The study was primarily a qualitative study (which is typically much harder to carry out than most quantitative studies), and lessons from the study are extremely rich.

I see The Jan Perspective throughout this entire article. First, the stance taken by the authors (researchers) is one of studying the dynamics of what *can* happen given the introduction of new technologies—where "what can happen" includes unintended and unplanned changes in students' and teachers' roles.

It is very easy to imagine research designs that would fail to capture these exciting kinds of unexpected changes. For example, the authors might have specified a set of clear, predefined goals for Internet use and measured only whether students did or did not meet them. This approach could easily have failed to capture numerous unintended changes such as the increases in student autonomy, and the warmer and less adversarial relationships between teachers and students. Overall, the approach taken by Schofield and Davidson allowed them to gather evidence for a principle long held by Jan and others (e.g., Hativa, 1994); namely, that "computers are not just tools that perform expected functions in classrooms in completely predictable ways" (e.g., Schofield & Davidson, this issue).

The Jan Perspective is also relevant to the attitudes of the teachers who were involved in the Internet studies. It takes courage to implement practices that may well take teachers out of their comfort zones. These comfort zones involve much more than feeling at ease with the technology, although that is part of the story. Schofield and Davidson provide numerous examples that illustrate how teachers had to change their roles and become learners who often relied on the expertise of their students. These are exactly the kinds of roles that Jan loved to promote.

Schofield and Davidson also suggest that some teachers seemed more prepared to deal with uncertainty and unintended outcomes than others. The same seemed to be true of students. Here is a case where an opportunity to learn about people such as Jan, and to explore the core values that appear to guide her willingness to take risks and learn from others, could serve as very valuable model for researchers, teachers and students alike. It represents an example of "people knowledge" that is discussed by Lin & Schwartz (this issue).

REFLECTION AT THE CROSSROAD OF CULTURES

Xiaodong Lin and Dan Schwartz's article is squarely in line with the Jan Perspective. Their title nicely captures one of Jan's core values, which involves relishing the opportunities for learning that stem from immersing oneself in social contexts that differ from one's own. Lin and Schwartz explore how this can be accomplished both in person and virtually.

Lin and Schwartz make the important point that mere contact with different cultures is far from sufficient for generating the kinds of learning that lead to understanding and appreciation. Their discussion of reflective adaptation is very important in this regard. "Without opportunities for reflective adaptive, people can become uncomprehending subordinates to practice or cynics stuck in ineffectual rejection" (Lin & Schwartz, this issue). They provide a very insightful analysis of reflection that integrates views from both the West and the East.

Lin and Schwartz also provide several examples of the importance of "humanizing culture" in order to help people move beyond stereotypes. Examples include providing people with stories of other peoples' experiences (e.g., The Strange Professor experiment; Lin & Bransford, 2001), and being honest about one's goals and doubts (e.g., the study where American students included self assessments of work they shared with Hong Kong students). A related strategy is to create opportunities for mutual learning by having people (e.g., United States and Hong Kong teachers) build something together. Participants collaborated in activities such as building internet-based lessons (e.g., in AdventureWorlds) to be co-taught to a diverse group of students. One of the important outcomes of these activities was an increased appreciation and respect for the contributions that others made.

There are many similarities between the virtual activities designed by Lin and Schwartz and the act of collaboratively building a Iu Mienh house (see Hammond, this issue). In both cases, it is the core values of The Jan Perspective that are foundational to the work.

SUMMARY AND THOUGHTS ABOUT NEXT STEPS

I am confident that Jan would be very happy with the articles in this issue. Each article yields many more insights than I have been able to discuss—my short commentaries do not do justice to them. Nevertheless, I hope I have been able to convey at least some of their strengths and show how their work differs from many other attempts to study issues of culture, human development and technology. In my opinion, all the contributors to this special issue work from a set of core values that are congruent with what I have called "The Jan Perspective." These values have profound effects on what is studied, how it is studied, and the conclusions one draws. Jan lived these values every day.

In my closing remarks I want to draw upon another important characteristic of Jan. She always asked "how can we do things better?" For example, how might studies of culture, development and technology be oriented in the future? I briefly mention four possible directions.

One is to combine the efforts of a number of individual studies (including those presented in this special issue) to generate a set of testable conjectures about methods of collaboration and reflection that can help members of the world community learn about one another in ways that go beyond simply "sampling their food" and memorizing facts about their forms of government, major exports, and lifestyles. The studies discussed in this special issue provide a number of powerful examples for mutual learning. Creating a broader and testable theoretical framework that has implications for an even wider range of particular examples appears to be both an important and feasible goal.

A second possible direction is explore the degree to which the kinds of values characteristic of "The Jan Perspective," and of the work discussed in this special issue, could help all students achieve at higher levels. These values include respecting people as having something to contribute rather than always looking for their deficits relative to mainstream culture (including school cultures), and actively searching for "funds of knowledge" (e.g., Lee, this issue) that can provide a basis for accelerating learning in a variety of content areas such as science, mathematics and literacy. There are important conjectures that student achievement can be accelerated if teachers know not only the content knowledge relevant to their discipline, but have also received in-depth training in working with students who come from other cultures or who have special needs (e.g., Haycock, 2001). This is an important line of research that needs further study. The contributors to this special issue could play a powerful role in this regard.

A third possibility for future directions is to explore in more detail the role of "shared personal histories" (sometimes called "people knowledge") in facilitating learning and collaboration. If we have tried our best to build a Iu Mienh house together, struggled to co-teach a virtual lesson in Adventure Worlds, worked together on an Internet project, a Jasper Adventure, Worldwatcher, and so forth, we share some personal experiences and know that we share them. These personal histories can help us formulate "the story behind the story" when we deal with one another. For example, they can help us overcome negative stereotypes and avoid unwarranted assumptions about one another's intentions. Lin and Schwartz (this issue) discuss the importance of "humanizing culture," and the development of "people knowledge" appears to be an important step in this direction. Given the knowledge, skills and stance toward research of each of the contributors to this special issue, I am confident that they could help us better understand the role that "people knowledge' plays in our lives.

A fourth possibility for future directions is to think beyond the traditional goals of formal schooling and help people learn to bridge the "economic divide" and find ways to help their own communities. The Nobel Prize winning economist Amartya Sen (1999) provided powerful arguments for a new perspective on economic development that helps people become more proactive participants in their own economic and political environments. Technology is playing a major role in this endeavor. For example, a micro-loan to a family in a rural Indian village can allow the family to rent a cell phone that they can then rent to other people who need information about crop prices, health care, and so forth (J. Foster, Personal Communication, December 14, 2001). The potentials are endless—both for other countries and here at home.

REFERENCES

Boykin, A. W. (1994). Harvesting culture and talent: African American children and educational reform. In R. Rossi (Ed.), *Educational reform and at risk students.* New York: Teachers College Press.

Bransford, J. D., Brown, A. L., & Cocking, R. R. (1999). *How people learn: Brain, mind, experience, and school.* Washington, DC: National Academy Press.

Cole, M. (1996). *Cultural psychology: A once and future discipline.* Cambridge, MA: Harvard University Press.

Hativa, N. (1994). What you design is not what you get (WYDINWYG): Cognitive, affective, and social impacts of learning with ILS—an integration of findings from six-years of qualitative and quantitative studies. *International Journal of Educational Research, 21*(1), 81–112.

Haycock, K. (2001). Closing the achievement gap. *Educational Leadership, 58*(6), 6.

Lin, X. D., & Bransford, J. D. (2001). *People knowledge: A missing ingredient in many of our educational designs.* Unpublished manuscript. Nashville, TN: Vanderbilt University.

McAdoo, H. P., & McAdoo, J. L. (1985). *Black children: Social, educational and parental environments.* Beverly Hills, CA: Sage.

Nobles, W. (1980). African philosophy: Foundations for Black psychology. In R. L. Jone (Eds.), *Black psychology* (2nd ed., pp. 23–36). New York: Harper & Row.

Sen, A. (1999). *Development as freedom.* New York: Random House.

MIND, CULTURE, AND ACTIVITY, *10*(1), 86–89

Studying Complex Social Practice to Improve Lives: Humanistic Computing for Learning

Louis M. Gomez

Northwestern University

Roy Pea

Stanford University

The articles contained in this issue are an outstanding tribute to Jan Hawkins the scholar, the researcher, and the person. Like most special people Jan found many ways to have an impact on those around her. In commenting on the connection of these works and Jan's life we highlight three themes of her guiding ethos. As Jan did, the work in this issue urges us to consider the power of diversity to facilitate our understanding and improvement of the social world, the transformative nature of powerful tools on practice, and the reports described here place in stark relief the propositions that a commitment to improvement should lie at the very foundation of the science and research on teaching and learning. In the following paragraphs, we highlight each theme as it occurs in this issue and connect it to Jan's life and work. And, Roy reflects on how the settings he shared with Jan Hawkins, at Rockefeller University (1977–1979) and Bank Street College (1981–1986), provided important theoretical and methodological influences on her orientation that we can continue to learn from today.

As we look around today, we see attention to diversity, in early 21st century research and popular culture vacillating between two extremes. One the one hand, people of color, non-native speakers of English, and others who contribute to the full spectrum of life in the United States are treated as though they have some fundamental deficit for which education, teaching and learning or technology can make up. On the other hand, with a polite nod to political correctness, all diversity is said to be "respected" and "valued." In neither case is the genuine power of diversity explored as a lens to help us understand the human condition in general and problems in teaching and learning in particular. In this respect, the articles in this issue are a welcome breath of fresh air. The Linn and Schwartz article, for example, highlights how a core aspect of cognition, namely reflection, can be much better understood by exploring its practice across cultural contexts. Hammond's article provides an extraordinary example of an ethnographic study of community action. This article shows how the simple act of building a house is a powerful act of everyday cognition and, how that cognition, revealed, helps us understand how culture shapes our existence. Hammond highlights in her work how this act of building a house was an act of cultural commerce that highlighted differences in cultural contributions and served as a bridge between

Requests for reprints should be sent to Louis Gomez, School of Education and Social Policy, Northwestern University, 2115 North Campus Drive, Evanston, IL 60208. E-mail: lgomez@northwestern.edu

two communities. Like Jan Hawkins, these authors deeply appreciate the potential for understanding in day-to-day cognition, especially when we pay attention to how practice spans, and fails to span, cultural contexts.

The articles in this issue, especially those of Lee and of Schofield and Davidson, recognize the transformative power of technical tools to reshape the social context of learning. These articles fit well in the tradition that Jan Hawkins and others initiated in spurring a shift in our consideration of *understanding tools used in context* (in contrast to a focus on understanding tool use as a deviation from designers' intent). Jan and her colleagues conducted a group of formative studies that were instrumental in creating learner-appropriate activities for the first generation of multimedia curriculum design, published as the PBS series, *Voyage of the Mimi.* Jan's work helped us see that the issue of *mediation* was a central one. She encourages us to ask: how can the interface and teacher's support help guide a student to productive and engaging learning and work? Schofield and Davidson's report in this issue follows directly in this vein. Their article encourages us to see how powerful Internet tools help children and teachers forge new styles of interactive relationships with one another.

Jan's insights also helped the field to ask how the flexibility of new technologies can serve to mediate *learner's interpretations* of the representations and functions of tools or curriculum. Carol Lee's article is well aligned with this vital theme. In her article, Lee helps us understand that, through creative design and principled analysis, new technologies can be structured so that they connect more deeply to the day-to-day experiences in learning for children of color. Collectively, the chapters by Lee, and by Schofield and Davidson highlight the issue of designing for flexible adaptation of technologies to meet diverse classroom and cultural needs. Jan would have relished these efforts, as the viewpoint of empowering the users of technologies, rather than privileging the intent of the designers, was always her starting place. She would want to ask hard questions about what "flexibility" means here, and whether the people, using the tools, perceive the flexibility the designers seek.

Unlike the "technological determinism" that can bring a depressing fatalism to discourse and research on technologies and people, Jan was an optimist about the human condition, and the power of the human spirit to innovate, to connect, to explore and to find new pathways toward a reinvigoration of culture and the future in education. "Can't we make it better?" She would ask. "How can we find new tasks to uncover under- appreciated capabilities of learners?" It is worthwhile highlighting some of the fertile ground that contributed to this orientation. In 1980, Jan Hawkins came to Bank Street College of Education in New York City, across the city from Columbia University, to begin her work on educational computing. Her orientation, when she was working with Joe Glick in the developmental psychology doctoral program at the Graduate Center of the City University of New York, was that of a developmental psychologist prepared in a sociocultural tradition. Just prior to this period, she had been regularly immersed in the late 1970s in the Institute for Comparative Human Development[1] at Rockefeller University, where Joe brought his graduate students for the lively culture that was established in those halls off York Avenue when Michael Cole, (the late) Sylvia Scribner, Ray McDermott, William Hall, Lois Hood and others were working on an invigorating landscape of intellectual and empirical issues and dilemmas at the intersection of cognitive, developmental and cross-cultural psychology, cognitive

---

[1] In 1978 the Institute for Comparative Human Development was closed. Michael Cole moved to the University of California, San Diego and established the Laboratory of Comparative Human Cognition

anthropology, and sociolinguistics—as the nexus of mind and society was explored, debated, and new positions were being defined. This was the era in which Scribner and Cole's (1981) *Psychology of Literacy* was being written, when Vygotsky's (1990) writings on *Mind in Society* were brought together and translated by Mike Cole and his colleagues, and when the LCHC newsletter was launched. It was an era when many of us were seeking to uncover children's unrecognized capabilities that were often masked due to the nature of the experimental task. This was a particular issue across cultures but also in developmental studies of reasoning.

It is essential to understand this heritage of ways of thinking about and exploring problems at the interface of mind, culture, reasoning, development, activity, language, and other representational forms to begin to understand Jan and her ways of thinking and working. Of course she brought to her life's work her unique spirit and ways of being that probably attracted her to the CUNY program to begin with, but we can find many ways in which this CUNY-Rockefeller period contributed to her theoretical dispositions, the kinds of questions she asked, and the participants' point of view that she always sought to establish. Understanding the meaning of "the experimental situation" from the participant's view was a key strategy in the cross-cultural studies that Cole, Glick, and Scribner had pioneered in their research and this decentering and empathetic move lived at the heart of Jan's intellectual and personal style throughout her career. Jan's acute respect for diversity in values and perspectives, as they arise in the contexts of education and computing across contexts, institutions, and culture reflects this keystone commitment.

Jan brought these views to bear in the struggles we and others had together while tackling the problems of how to think about and study the introduction, uses, and outcomes of computers in elementary school classrooms and teaching practices around Logo programming and, later, many other introductions of computing for learning in the Bank Street School, which is where our collaborative work began in 1981. This was an exotic new context as microcomputers entered the classroom for the first time. Here we had an extraordinarily powerful new symbol system—and children were going to control it with Logo, the programming language coupled with Seymour Papert's influential theory of learning change in *Mindstorms* (1982). How were developmental methods appropriate to uncovering children's thinking about how microcomputers create graphics from Logo programs, or in their social interactions around group work with these machines? What roles were the teachers playing as mediators of a new symbol system for the children, and how did these new activities relate to their own learning and role perceptions within the school and college? How might issues of gender differences in play work out in the "computer classroom"? What could we learn, from clinical interviewing, about children's conceptions of microcomputers and programming and what they were good for, and what was interesting or challenging to learn? How was the classroom changing? And how could we make it better for the learners and teachers?

Each in their own way the articles in this issue encourage us all to ask, and to continue to ask, "can't we make it better?" Jan's work, and the work contained in this issue, reminds us that the most important reason we do what we do is to improve the life chances of people. Toward the end of her life, Jan was a realist about how hard systems are to change. But she was, like the authors in this issue, fundamentally committed to the proposition that "change, they must." Like Hawkins, the authors in this issue have sought to find new designs to uncover under-appreciated potential in people by careful attention to culture and diversity, rich analysis of social practice, and looking to how the affordances of technologies can enrich this action agenda. Here we find in each of the chapters something unexpected about the transformations of human interactions in the spaces of learning with technologies and other mediators. As we remember Jan we warmly recall that she always sought to be a mediator between different disciplines, between teachers and administrators, and between instructional and technology designers. The authors of these chapters carry on this tradition in their work of building bridges that will improve lives.

REFERENCES

Papert, S. (1982). *Mindstorm: Children, computers, and powerful ideas.* New York: Basic Books.
Scribner, S., & Cole, M. (1981). *The psychology of Literacy.* Cambridge, MA: Harvard University Press.
Vygotsky, L. (1990). *Mind in society.* Cambridge, MA: Harvard University Press.

MIND, CULTURE, AND ACTIVITY, *10*(1), 90–92

Remembering Jan Hawkins

Margaret Honey

Education Development Center, Inc.

Allan Collins

School of Education
Northwestern University

Spanning more than 2 decades, the work of Jan Hawkins has had a profound impact on the technology and education field. Jan began her career in educational technology as a founding member of the Center for Children and Technology. In 1991 she became the Director of the Center. In September 1999 Jan joined the faculty of the Harvard Graduate School of Education, and continued to codirect the Center for Children and Technology until her death in the winter of 1999. Her intellectual handprint on our work in the learning sciences field is unmistakable.

Jan was deeply interested in issues of cultural diversity, and spent much of her career exploring the ways in which technologies are interpreted and appropriated in varying cultural contexts. In part, what motivated Jan's unwavering commitment to these issues was a deeply held personal desire that drove her to seek the unexpected in the unfamiliar. In the mid-1980s Jan decided she was going to learn to fly and she subsequently traveled from the East coast to Alaska in a single engine plane. What she loved most about this experience was her encounters with the people she met at tiny airfields that dotted her journey west. She described her trip as a continual process of being pulled into other worlds. This is how Jan most valued learning—through encounters with the unanticipated that would allow her to shift her frame of reference and see the world through a different lens.

Much of Jan's work, particularly in later years focused on issues of complexity and on the dilemmas that one encounters when introducing novel practices into established institutional structures. Understanding the nature of these dilemmas was at the center of Jan's analysis of both the possibilities and limitations of using educational technology to facilitate change.

In one of her last pieces of writing—a article aptly titled "Dilemmas"—Jan reflects back on 2 decades of experimentation centered on the role of technology in education. She does in this text what she always did best in person—hold together the tensions that surface between the potential of educational technologies and the reality of a system of schooling that has been and continues to be remarkably resistant to change.

Jan was allergic to uniform, overly optimistic and simplistic interpretations. Jan cultivated an eclectic understanding of phenomena and she always insisted on the relevance of context to this

Requests for reprints should be sent to Margaret Honey, Education Development Center, Inc., 96 Morton Street, New York, NY 10014. E-mail: mhoney@edc.org

process. In many respects Jan was the opposite of a successful academic researcher. She never defined a single body of work as her own, or cultivated a uniform relationship to theory, and she spent much of her time convincing others that her ideas were theirs.

Jan held steady to a vision of effective learning. She believed that students needed to be actively engaged in meaningful tasks. She believed that education should be personal and teachers should work in environments that allow them to know children well. She believed in the promise of collaborations between learners and experts, and in the culture of apprenticeships in which students are deeply immersed in the practices and habits that define a field of inquiry. And Jan believed that children should be inspired learners.

One of her favorite anecdotes from the early days of research on the *Voyage of the Mimi* was the passion a young student displayed when he tried to reenact a scene from the video. In this episode the archeologists who are diving for Mayan artifacts off the coast of Mexico come across a Mayan stele—an ancient stone monument—that is partially buried in sand under many feet of water. Their challenge is to raise this 800-pound slab of stone to the surface. They devise a strategy in which they attach garbage bags to the four corners of the monument and then inflate the bags with air from their dive tanks. A fifth grader in one of the schools where we were working—using a combination of brick, Baggies, and a straw as an air hose—tried to recreate the entire scene in his bathtub.

The point for Jan, of course, was not whether he succeeded or failed, but that he was inspired to try and his teacher could build on his passion.

Jan's work with schools brought her into close contact with both possibility and limitations. She was deeply influenced by the work of Ted Sizer and Debbie Meier and spent a fair amount of time at the Central Park East Schools in the 1980s. These are small schools in which teachers know their students well. These are schools where students' interests and questions drive the process of deep and sustained inquiry—the kinds of places that prize bathtub experimentation.

Most schools aren't structured to support this kind of learning. Transmission, not inquiry, remains the dominant instructional paradigm, and Jan believed that people don't learn much of lasting use and significance through the direct transmission of information. This is the first dilemma that she speaks about in her article.

A second dilemma that Jan acknowledged centered on dissemination. Jan believed that whereas model programs, model schools, model classrooms can serve as images of change, that the real work of reform involves rethinking at the local level. The process of adaptation through experimentation and interpretation—or what Nora Sabelli calls the localization of innovation—is critical to the work of reform. And yet, in so much of our reform work we leave out this critical step. Jan saw great promise in the standards movement and in efforts like New American Schools, and yet she recognized that the promise of both learning and systemic reform would not be realized unless we made room for interpretation and enactment in the local context.

A third dilemma is one that still surrounds us in the unrealized promise of educational technology. Jan was one of what was then a relatively small community of researchers working during the 1980s to bring technological tools to the classroom. Jan believed that technologies could provide powerful scaffolds to complex processes like inquiry and computational reasoning and the interpretation of media artifacts. Yet, she realized in the course of her work that school contexts are powerful mediators and frequently powerful resisters of learning innovations. More often than not technological innovations are appropriated to existing paradigms of teaching and learning.

Although the new technologies—the communication and information affordances of the Internet—promise heretofore impossible opportunities for schools—Jan asked simply: Do we really mean it? Do we want to embrace complexity, rethink and reshape teachers' jobs, create environments that are genuine learning communities, and educate students to participate in a world that is truly global?

The articles in this special issue would have given Jan heart. They continue to wrestle with these questions and they explore issues of collaboration that push us toward the "yes" end of this question. One of the things that Jan believed in deeply is that technologies should be used broadly to invite student engagement and facilitate the creative expression of ideas. And one of the things that drew many of us to embrace her work was her belief that technologies afford learners powerful opportunities for expression. The articles in this issue examine how technologies can support issues of engagement, expression, and change across different cultural contexts and practices. Jan would embrace the work represented in this issue as capturing what she most valued—an exploration of how technologies can be used to provide people with the opportunity to think deeply, express ideas, and share their thinking with others in ways that give rise to new perspectives and possibilities.

MIND, CULTURE, AND ACTIVITY, *10*(1), 93–97

BOOK REVIEW

Alexander Luria and the Cultural–Historical Activity Theory: Pieces for the History of An Outstanding Collaborative Project in Psychology

Alexander Romanovich Luria, A Scientific Biography, by E. D. Homskaya, New York: Kluwer Academic/Plenum, 2001, 190 pp., $49.50.

Reviewed by
Anna Stetsenko
City University of New York
Graduate Center

This book's appearance is extremely timely—it coincides with the 2002 centennial of Alexander Luria's birth. The life and scientific heritage of this Russian scholar have been widely celebrated, with several international conferences held to commemorate Luria's achievements, including one in Moscow organized by his many students and followers, now renowned scholars themselves, working in various institutions in Moscow and around the world.

The book that is now available for the English-speaking readers in translation from Russian (the original was published in 1992), is written by Evgenija Davydovna Homskaya—one of the closest students and colleagues of Luria who came to be a prominent neuropsychologist herself, having authored a number of important publications (both with Luria and on her own) and taught many generations of students at the Moscow State Lomonosov University (including the author of this review). Homskaya, who continues her work and teaching today, wrote this book, in her own words, to honor the memory of her beloved teacher, colleague, and friend. The book by Homskaya represents a valuable source of information about this prominent scholar of the 20th century and a unique addition to the existing literature in that it provides a glimpse at Luria's life and work from within the immediate context of his investigative project and scientific path as it unfolded during the many years of a close collaboration between Luria and Homskaya.

The book should be of interest to a broad audience of psychologists for several reasons. First, Alexander Luria's life is remarkable in and of itself. He represented a rare breed of scientists with a uniquely broad, almost encyclopedic, knowledge and expertise in fields as diverse as biology, psychiatry, anthropology, medicine, physiology, neurophysiology, psychology, forensic science,

Requests for reprints should be sent to Anna Stetsenko, City University of New York, Graduate Center, 365 Fifth Avenue, New York, NY 10016. E-mail: astetsenko@gc.cuny.edu

and linguistics. His achievements are remarkable in most of these fields and in this breadth of interests and achievements Luria can be compared to the most brilliant scholars in the history of civilization. It is remarkable that he achieved so much against the many odds and hurdles brought about by the cultural-historical circumstances of his life time. Indeed, Luria's life coincided with the most dramatic and often tragic events in modern history. He was only 12 when Russia joined the World War I in 1914, followed by the Bolshevik revolution that dismantled practically all existing societal institutions and unleashed a brutal civil war, soon to be followed by a repressive totalitarian regime. As if this wasn't enough, Luria also lived through the most devastating years of the World War II that caused enormous troubles and demanded almost inhumane sacrifice from all citizens of the Soviet Union (including a sacrifice of 20 million people who perished in the fight against fascism). It is only after Stalin's death and with the end of mass repressions, when Luria was already in his mid-50s, that certain degree of normalcy has been achieved in the Soviet Union, and Luria enjoyed some peaceful and productive 20 years of his later career. He died in 1977, only 10 years before another dramatic turn of events that his country again would go through with the advent of the Gorbachev's perestrojka. Luria no doubt would have welcomed the changes toward openness and intellectual freedom instigated by perestrojka, and moreover, he was one of those many Russians who had themselves prepared and made possible the peaceful transformation of the Soviet Union. Luria was also a talented and inspiring teacher, beloved by many generations of his students who are now proudly continuing his approach in psychology. Quite remarkably, Luria was, by all accounts, a person of a robust vitality and great ambitions that he employed in the interest of science that he selflessly served all his life. He was also an optimist at heart, full of enthusiasm and joy (it is hard to come across Luria's photo without this beaming infectious smile of his), in one word, a happy man—something obvious even to those who, like myself, had a privilege of knowing him only very briefly. I personally believe that Luria's exceptional accomplishments and high spirit in the face of adversity were made possible by the fact that he had devoted his life to a meaningful and socially significant goal—the goal that became embodied in the *leading activity* that organized and underpinned both his life and scholarly work. It is this puzzle of how a human being can withstand and even thrive, to an extraordinary degree, in the face of seismic changes and often catastrophic events that makes the book about Luria so fascinating, I would expect, for a rather wide readership. Indeed, a look at life and work of a scholar of his rank and his fate reminds us of the limitlessness of human potential. It also reminds us of how trivial are those theories and views that link human well-being and happiness to the selfish pragmatic of any sort, or to the benevolence of life circumstances as a prerequisite for happiness. I think that Homskaya's book very convincingly conveys this baffling paradox of Luria's outstanding scholarly feat and challenges many preconceptions about human creativity and life.

At another level, the book by Homskaya is clearly of interest to anyone concerned with the history and major principles of neuropsychology—a discipline that Luria founded by bringing the study of the brain and the psychological processes together. Luria's unique approach to the problem of how mind and brain are related was based on the innovative ideas that brain mechanisms (a) serve as an instrument for carrying out meaningful goal-directed activities, (b) are formed in the real life context of each individual's development in response to the demands of this real life context, and (c) are shaped in important ways by cultural artifacts such as language. Although seemingly simple, these ideas de facto signified a completely new path for studying the old mysteries of mind, enabling Luria to make a whole array of important discoveries about how the brain works and to formulate many ground breaking principles of its development (e.g., the principle of the dynamic systemic localization of brain functions). To this day, these discoveries and principles constitute the cutting edge in neurosciences; in fact, they considerably presaged what has been recently widely disseminated in the media as the greatest discovery of the 20th century, namely, that brain functioning can be sustained, even in very old age, and new brain cells can grow in response to individual's active engagement in activities, thus likening the brain to a sort of a "muscle," the strength and vitality of which depend on how much it is made use of (e.g., Kolata, 1998). Careful reconstruction and insightful explanation of Luria's achievements in neuropsychology constitutes perhaps the strongest feature of Homskaya's book, reflecting her own exceptional expertise in this field.

However, as Homskaya rightfully emphasizes in her book, Luria's contribution is not limited to neuropsychology. Instead, the real significance of Luria's studies is much broader in that they constitute an insightful and creative expansion, especially into the brain-and-mind area, of the cultural-historical school of thought with its broad implications for practically all significant matters in psychology. Homskaya, like most of her colleagues in Russia but only few authors in the West (with few notable exceptions, such as Michael Cole and James Wertsch, e.g., see Cole & Wertsch, 1996), regards Luria as the founder of the Vygotsky-Leont'ev-Luria approach in psychology. In several places throughout the book some important interdependencies and continuities in thinking among all of these three scholars are highlighted and discussed.

In this respect, the book about Luria should be of interest to anyone who wants to better understand the history of psychology at large, and thus to better grasp the present state of this discipline as well as the possible directions for its future growth. Although Vygotsky's heritage has now become an integral part of contemporary psychological discourse, the cultural-historical school of thought *as a whole*, represented by several generations of psychologists such as Luria, who participated both in its inception and its development and expansion during the many decades after Vygotsky's death, still remains insufficiently understood and reflected upon in today's psychology. Vygotsky is often portrayed as a scholar who alone created the cultural-historical approach in a solitary pursuit of abstract theoretical principles, and his close collaboration with Leont'ev, Luria and other members of his very close team is, for the most part, only briefly mentioned in the literature devoted to Vygotsky (e.g., Valsiner & van der Veer, 2000; van der Veer & Valsiner, 1991). Yet attempts to understand cultural-historical approach are incomplete if one disregards the complex dynamics of how this approach emerged and developed as an essentially *collaborative investigative project* that entailed truly collective efforts of a number of scholars committed to the same ideals and goals and set on the same agenda of developing psychology as an objective science capable of making a difference in the real world. In that sense, the cultural-historical theory represents an example of a genuine school in psychology, clearly rooted in a shared philosophical background and committed to common ideological, theoretical, and pragmatic ideals.

The reason why the collaborative and ideologically driven nature of the cultural-historical theory is so often disregarded in its contemporary accounts is the old, essentially mentalist, approach to the history of psychology as a *history of ideas produced by isolated individuals in their lonely pursuits of abstract truths* (even if intellectual interdependency among the ideas and "voices" of various scholars is admitted). This conception of history as a history of ideas that constitute a separate mental (ephemeral) reality isolated from much more palpable processes of *doing* science, inevitably, and unwarrantedly, excludes a host of other than mental processes from the scope of what is considered as belonging into the body of science and knowledge. Excluded are ideological and political influences, collaborative and participatory processes, and the *sociocultural context at large* (even if its impact, in an extraneous way, on the knowledge production is admitted) as legitimate constituents of the very fabric of science, as they become transposed into particular investigative projects and define its direction and its very nature. This conception of history follows on comfortably from the centuries old views on (a) science as a politics- and value-free enterprise separate from the practical and tangible processes of real life (if even applicable, at some points in time, to certain practical areas); and (b) knowledge as produced "in the heads" of individual scientists and belonging to the mental realm that is separate from (if even not completely unrelated to) the realm of practical transformative processes in the real world.

Unfortunately, Homskaya's book, although full of important insights and information, does not go far enough, in countering these traditional views on science and knowledge. Moreover, Homskaya herself, in those rare instances when she hints at the type of meta-theory that she employed to reconstruct Luria's heritage, subscribes to the view that, "the history of science is a chain consisting of individual links, histories of particular scientists" (p. 117). In a way, Homskaya focused more on Luria as a "particular scientist" than on "the chain," that is, the collaborative project that Luria belonged to and that his life and work has come to embody. That this is the case is strikingly clear in that Homskaya herself, as an important colleague and follower of Luria, who spent at least 25 years working closely together with him, is nowhere to be found in the book. How did she come to know Luria; what forms did their collaboration take and how did it evolve; what kind of conflicts (perhaps), disagreements and shared political views (if any), practical agendas and so on, were involved—these are the kinds of issues that are not addressed in the book. Within the traditionally mentalist view on the history of psychology, this clearly is a testament to the author's commendable desire to stay in the shadow of the giant and timidly conceal one's own participation in how Luria's path in psychology evolved. Within this traditional view such matters are simply of no relevance, deserving only a brief mention, because they do not belong into the body of knowledge. However, these omissions, together with the fact that Luria's collaboration with Vygotsky and other members of the cultural-historical school, as well as Luria's views on matters beyond psychology (e.g., on politics and ideology) are only sketched, are regrettable.

They are particularly regrettable if one wants to embark on a journey to reconstruct the dynamics of the cultural-historical school as a *collaborative, multi-generational, value-laden, and ideologically- driven investigative project that stretched far beyond the confines of science in its traditional mentalist guise.* The history of this project has still to be written in a way that would reflect and employ the recent breakthroughs in the meta-theoretical approaches to the history of science (e.g., Danziger, 1990; Knorr-Certina, 1981; Morawski, 1994). Even more important, this history is still to be written in a way that would employ the insights of the cultural-historical school itself—insights about the nature of science and human knowledge as forms of essentially practical, purposeful and goal-directed activity that are shaped, at each and every step of their development, by the very goals that they purport to achieve (e.g., Stetsenko, 1986; 1990). Such history of the Vygotsky-Leont'ev-Luria school would have to reveal how the cultural-historical context of their work, specifically the revolutionary project of changing society based on ideals of equality and social justice that these scholars clearly espoused (all the subsequent dramatic failings of this project notwithstanding), instead of being an outside source of influence, became integrated *right into the body* of their work, into its methodology, and the very knowledge it produced. Such a historical account would substantially alter the landscape of what is now portrayed as the history of psychology in the 20th century, as it would reveal how one direction in this discipline has been developed based on *ideals and goals of human liberation and social transformation*. It is this commitment to the broader transformative—liberational social project that puts the cultural-historical approach into stark opposition to much of alternative developments in the 20th century, be it behaviorism with its overarching pursuit of controlling human behavior or cognitive psychology with its commitment to a value-free science model and related pursuit of universal and often "ameaningful" psychological principles (cf., Koch, 1999; cited in Smith, 2001). It is this commitment of the cultural-historical approach to such radical social project that sheds light on so many of its pivotal elements (e.g., its totally nontraditional view of theory as being a living instrument and form of practice), marks its unique standing in the history of psychology, and ultimately explains its otherwise startling appeal to so many scholars today (especially those scholars, I believe, who feel the urgent need for social changes and want to transform psychology into an instrument of such changes).

Such a historical account is a formidable task, likely demanding also a collective effort by many scholars, and it would be naive to expect it to be resolved in the present book. Homskaya made a marvelous job at presenting an important, though fractional, piece of the cultural-historical puzzle of how the cultural-historical school in psychology emerged and developed in the great political schisms of ideals and reality of its time. All the above mentioned limitations of the book notwithstanding, they do not undermine its general value and Evegenia Davydovna Homskaya deserves great credit not only for having written this book but also for continuing and expanding, now into the next century and against the odds of new challenges facing Russia today (e.g., the commercialization of psychology that pushes it away from ideals that the cultural-historical psychology stands for), the project and mission of her great colleague and teacher, Alexander Luria.

REFERENCES

Cole, M., & Wertsch, J. (1996). *Contemporary implications of Vygotsky and Luria* (Heinz Werner Lecture Series, Vo. XXI). Worcester, MA: Clark University.

Danziger, K. (1990). *Constructing the subject: Historical origins of psychological research*. New York: Cambridge University Press.

Koch, S. (1999). Ameaning in the humanities. In S. Koch, *Psychology in human context: Essays in dissidence and reconstruction* (D. Finkelman & F. Kessel, Eds.; pp. 267–290). Chicago: University of Chicago Press.

Kolata, G. (1998, March 17). Studies find brain grows new cells. *New York Times*, Sec. F, p. 1.

Knorr-Certina, K. D. (1981). *The manufacture of knowledge: An essay on the constructivist and contextualist nature of science*. New York: Pergamon.

Morawski, J. (1994). *Practicing feminism, reconstructing psychology. Notes on a liminal science*. Ann Arbor: University of Michigan Press.

Smith, M. B. (2001). Sigmund Koch as critical humanist. *American Psychologist, 56*, 441–444.

Stetsenko, A. (1986). Issledovatelskaja zadacha i struktura psihologicheskogo znanija [Research goal and the structure of psychological knowledge]. In A. Barabanchikov (Ed.), *Metodologija psihologicheskogo issledovanija* [*Meta-theory and methods of psychological research*] (pp. 10–23). Moscow: USSR Academy of Sciences Press.

Stetsenko, A. (1990). O roli i statuse metodologicheskogo znanija v sovremennoj Sovetskoj psihologii [The role and status of meta- theoretical knowledge in contemporary Soviet psychology]. *Vestnik Moskovskogo Universiteta: Serija Psihologija* [*Journal of Moscow State University: Psychological Series*], *2*, 39–49.

Valsiner, J., & van der Veer, R. (2000). *The social mind: Construction of the idea*. Cambridge, England: Cambridge University Press.

van der Veer, R., & Valsiner, J. (1991). *Understanding Vygotsky: A quest for synthesis*. Oxford, England: Blackwell.

NOTES TO CONTRIBUTORS

If your work has important implications for characterizing the way people use their minds and organize their lives, we encourage you to submit an article for consideration. We are especially interested in articles that illuminate the relationship among the three categories that are on the masthead (mind, culture, and activity).

We consider two classes of articles: "substantial contributions" (20–30 pages) that present syntheses of theoretical and empirical research devoted to a significant topic and "thought pieces" (6–15 pages) that present new ideas, methods, points of view, and challenging data. We also include book reviews and shorter book notes. Please keep in mind when you are preparing a manuscript that our readership is unusually broad (anthropologists, psychologists, linguists, sociologists, educators, and public policy people are all among our subscribers); please avoid jargon that is familiar only to researchers in one field.

All submissions will be blind reviewed. To facilitate the blind reviewing, a separate cover page with the title, author's name, affiliation, electronic mail address, and telephone and fax numbers must accompany each manuscript. This information should not appear anywhere else on the manuscript.

Manuscripts should be prepared according to the *Publication Manual of the American Psychological Association* (5th ed.). An abstract of 100–150 words should be included on a separate page. All text, including indented matter, footnotes, and references, should be typed double-spaced on 8½ × 11 in. paper. The number and length of footnotes should be kept to a minimum. Footnotes should be numbered serially and included after the references in the text. All figures must be camera ready. Send submissions in triplicate to The Editors; Mind, Culture, and Activity; Centre for Sociocultural and Activity Theory Research; The School of Education; The University of Birmingham; Birmingham B15 2TT; United Kingdom.

MANUSCRIPT ACCEPTANCE AND COMPUTER DISKS: Authors of accepted manuscripts must submit (a) a disk containing two files (word-processor, preferably WordPerfect, and ASCII versions of the final version of the manuscript), (b) a printed copy of the final version of the manuscript, (c) camera-ready figures, (d) copies of all permissions obtained to reprint or adapt material from other sources, and (e) copyright-transfer agreement signed by all coauthors. (Note: Contact author must ascertain that all coauthors approve the accepted manuscript and concur with its publication in the journal.) The content of disk files must exactly match that of the manuscript copy, or there will be a delay in publication. Manuscripts and disk are not returned.

PRODUCTION NOTES: Authors' files are copyedited and typeset into page proofs. Contact authors bear sole responsibility for reading proofs to correct errors and answer editors' queries; authors may order reprints of their articles when they receive the proofs.

COPYRIGHT

For Product Safety Concerns and Information please contact our
EU representative GPSR@taylorandfrancis.com Taylor & Francis
Verlag GmbH, Kaufingerstraße 24, 80331 München, Germany